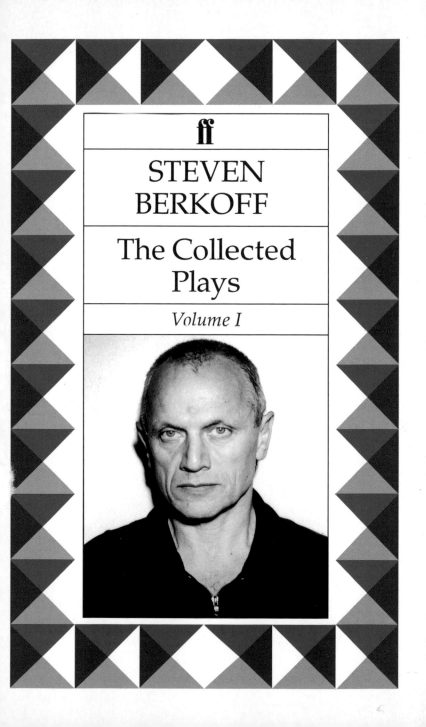

ff

STEVEN
BERKOFF

The Collected
Plays

Volume I

THE COLLECTED PLAYS
VOLUME I

THE COLLECTED PLAYS

VOLUME I

faber and faber

LONDON · BOSTON

This collection
first published in 1994
by Faber and Faber Limited
3 Queen Square London WC1N 3AU

East was first published in 1977 by John Calder (Publishers) Ltd, London
West was first published in *West and other plays* in 1985
by Faber and Faber Limited
Greek was first published privately by the author
1980 and then 1982 by John Calder (Publishers) Ltd, London
Sink the Belgrano! was first published in 1987
by Faber and Faber Limited
Lunch was first published in 1985
by Faber and Faber Limited

Photoset in Plantin by Parker Typesetting Service, Leicester
Printed in England by Clays Ltd, St Ives plc

British Library Cataloguing in Publication data is available

ISBN 0–571–16903–1

2 4 6 8 10 9 7 5 3

CONTENTS

EAST

*Elegy for the East End
and its energetic waste*

CHARACTERS

DAD
MUM
SYLV
LES
MIKE

AUTHOR'S NOTE

This play was written to exorcize certain demons struggling within me to escape. *East* takes place within my personal memory and experience and is less a biographical text than an outburst or revolt against the sloth of my youth and a desire to turn a welter of undirected passion and frustration into a positive form. I wanted to liberate that time squandered and sometimes enjoyed into a testament to youth and energy. It is a scream or a shout of pain. It is revolt. There is no holding back or reserve in the East End of youth as I remember . . . you lived for the moment and vitally held it . . . you said what you thought and did what you felt. If something bothered you, you let it out as strongly as you could, as if the outburst could curse and therefore purge whatever it was that caused it. One strutted and posed down the Lyceum Strand, the Mecca of our world, performed a series of rituals that let people know who and what you were, and you would fight to the death to defend that particular life style that was your own. *East* could be the east side of any city where the unveneered blast off at each other in their own compounded argot as if the ordinary language of polite communication was as dead as the people who uttered it. I stylized the events further by some cross-fertilization with Shakespeare and threw in a few classical allusions – this seemed to help to take it out further into a ritual and yet defined it with a distinct edge. It still felt like *East* and could not have been done, I believe, in any other dialect or accent except perhaps East Side New York. The acting has to be loose and smacking of danger . . . it must smart and whip out like a fairy's wicked lash. There is no reserve and therefore no embarrassment. One critic described it as 'filthy beyond the call of duty' but in fact it is a loving appreciation of the male and female form. We played it in three theatres starting at the small Traverse, Edinburgh, and it was good to hear the kind of laughter that came not only from the belly but had that ring of familiarity, that sudden explosive yelp of identification, when they laughed hardest, the dirty beasts.

East was first performed at the Traverse Theatre by the London Theatre Group for the 1975 Edinburgh Festival which then transferred to the King's Head, London. The cast was as follows:

DAD	Barry Stanton
MUM	Robert Longden
SYLV	Anna Nygh
LES	Barry Philips
MIKE	Steven Berkoff
Music	John Prior
Producer	Steven Berkoff

This version of *East* was first performed at the Greenwich Theatre in July 1976. The cast was as follows:

DAD	Matthew Scurfield
MUM	David Delve
SYLV	Anna Nygh
LES	Barry Philips
MIKE	Steven Berkoff
Music	Neil Hansford
Producer	Steven Berkoff

A new production of *East* was presented at the Regent Theatre in August 1977.

SCENE I

The stage is bare but for five chairs in a line upstage whereby the cast act as chorus for the events that are spoken, mimed and acted. A piano just offstage creates mood, adds tension and introduces themes. A large screen upstage centre has projected on it a series of real East End images, commenting and reminding us of the actual world just outside the stage. The cast enter and sit on five chairs facing front – piano starts up and they sing 'My Old Man says Follow the Van' – out of order and in canons and descants. It comes suddenly to a stop, MIKE *and* LES *cross to two oblong spots – image of two prisoners photographed for the criminal hall of fame. They pose three times before speaking.*

LES: Donate a snout, Mike?

MIKE: OK I'll bung thee a snout, Les.

MIKE: ⎱
LES: ⎰ Now you know our names.

MIKE: Mike's OK. After the Holy Saint . . . Mike with a hard K. Like a kick-swift . . . not mad about Les.

LES: It's soft, it's gooey . . . but choose it I did not . . . in my mother's hot womb did she curse this name on me . . . it's my handle . . . under the soft – it's spiky, under the pillow it's sharp . . . concealed instrument . . . offensive weapon lies waiting.

MIKE: Oh, he doth bestride Commercial Road like a Colossus . . . that's my manor . . . where we two first set our minces on each other . . . and those Irish yobs walk under our huge legs and peep about for dishonourable bother . . . he's my mucker, china or mate.

LES: And he mine since those days at least twelve moons ago when sailing out the Black Raven pub in Whitechapel the selfsame street where blessed Jack did rip and tear in cold thick nights so long ago . . . those muffled screams and slicing flesh no more than sweetest memories of him that went so humble 'bout his nightly graft. Tell how it chanced that we sworn mates were once the deadly poison of each other's eye.

7

MIKE: He clocked the bird I happened to be fiancéd to, my
    darling Sylv (of legendary knockers) and I doth take it
    double strong that this long git in suede and rubber, pimples
    sprouting forth like buttercups on sunny days from off his
    greasy boat: that he should dare to lay upon her svelte and
    tidy form his horror leering jellies . . . so I said to him 'fuck
    off thou discharge from thy mother's womb before with
    honed and sweetened razor I do trouble to remove thy balls
    from thee.'

LES: Oh! Ho! I gushed. You fancied me around the back with
    boots and chains and knives, behind the super cinema it was
    then called afore it came a cut-price supermarket (which we
    have well and truly robbed since then). So round the back we
    went that night . . . the fog was falling fast, our coat collars
    were up . . . our breath like dragon's steam did belch forth
    from our violent mouths . . . while at the selfsame time we
    uttered uncouth curses, thick with bloody and unholy
    violence of what we would most like to carve upon each
    other's skulls . . . the crowd of yobs that formed a ring of
    yellow faces in the lamplight.

MIKE: Right.

LES: . . . Hungry for the blood of creatures nobler and more
    daring than themselves.

MIKE: Right.

LES: With dribble down their loathsome mouths they leered and
    lusted for our broken bottles and cold steel to start the
    channels gouging in our white and precious cheeks.

MIKE: I thought now fuck this for a laugh.

LES: That's right.

MIKE: So what if sly old Sylv had led me on a touch by showing
    out to all the lads, provoking hard-ons and gang wars
    between opposing tribes from Hoxton to Tottenham . . .
    from Bethnal Green to Hornsey Town from Poplar up to
    Islington. The clash of steel and crunch of boot on testicle
    has long disturbed the citizens of those battle-scarred manors
    and blue-bottles with truncheons hard as iron have had their
    helmets (and their heads) sometimes removed by rude and

lusty lads complete with knuckle-dusters and iron bars
nicked from their dads.

LES: Any old iron.

MIKE: Honest and trusty trade upon the streets.

MIKE: ⎫
LES: ⎬ We thought now fuck this for a laugh!

LES: But we could hardly turn back now with five and fifty chinas
egging us on there, with shouts of 'come on Les, cut off his
cock', and 'punch the fucker's head in.'

LES: Or destroy him Mike . . . for fuck's sake don't just stand
there . . . nut him in the nose . . . and part his skull from him
the greasy turd and yaroo! Yarah! Use your iron . . . put the
boot in with shrieks of 'bollocks, slerp! Dog face and fucking
hell' . . . 'smash, hit, shithead' . . . 'anoint the cunt with
death' one cried (with voice so vehement). Oh Sylv, it was
thee, yes, thy gentle voice did sway me finally to deal out
pain, then in I went like paste. I flashed my raziory which
danced about his face like fireflies, reflecting in the cold wet
streets the little yellow gas light, till the sheet of red that splat
from out his pipes did dull it . . . just felt that soft thud,
thwat, as knife hits flesh . . . You know the feel? It's soft and
hard at once and gives you collywobbles with thrilldoms of
pure joy.

LES: My pure and angel face, my blessed boat did, on that sacred
night receive his homage . . . red did flow – I knew my cheek
was gaping open like a flag . . . but never mind, to stop the
Tiber, stop myself from kissing death flush on the lips I held
it with my hand, held what I could while trickling through
my fingers ran my juices sweet as life (*Murmurs of* 'brave Les'
. . . 'hard man', *etc*) and then I simply said 'you cunt'. Just
that. 'You cunt . . . I'll shit down scorpions of pain upon thee
. . . I'll eat you! Get it!!!' My iron found his skull where he
had just begun to move but left enough for me to bang and
crack a dash, enough bone there to bend and shift a bit . . .
split off and splinter bits in brain . . . his brain . . . splatter
. . . the lads said 'oink and assholes fucking hell! Too far
thou'rt gone and really farted death on him . . . Oh shit . . .

9

swerp . . . ugh . . . AAAAAARH . . . have it away, before
the law doth mark us for accessory.'

MIKE: So off they flew . . . left me for dead and Les near dying too
in pools of his own blood he lay choked . . . the steel had bit
too deep . . . I felt the silence creeping in . . . and found
myself in an old movie, silent like . . . and flickering to its
end . . . so what? (What's it all about?) Those cunts have left
us, shit in pants (their own) while we slosh round in guts . . .
they watched, were nicely freckled by our gore, and thought
'Let's scarper now, we had our fun, those cunts are done . . .
let's piss off 'fore the law should stride with boots hobnailed
in woe to grab us in their fat and gnarled claws.'

LES: We picked ourselves and all our bits from off the deck and
fell into each other's arms . . . with 'What the fuck', and
flashed a quirky red-soaked grin at our daft caper thinking
what a bloody sight . . . we can't jump on the 19 bus in our
condition looking like what they hang up in Smithfields . . .
Those bloody sides of beef (for those of thee unversed in the
geography of our fair state) so we did crawl and hop . . .
stagger and slide 'hold on Mike, nearly there . . . don't die in
Balls Pond Road you berk . . . grip hard' . . . I only had a
pint or two of rosy red in my tired veins myself . . . the rest I
used to paint the town with . . . would I have strength
enough to get there with my new-found mate, whose brains
were peeping out the top of his broke patch . . . would I not
conk out in the street at Aldgate East (untimely end dear Les
of youthful folly) our mums and dads with bellow, whine and
oily tears at our sad stones . . . we had those visions come and
go . . . they'd tell sad stories of the death of kids who lived
not wisely but too well.

MIKE: We were in love the time we stumbled into the casualty at
Charing Cross. And fell into the arms of white-gloved saints
who sewed a nifty stitch or ten . . . no questions asked and
when John Law did come and mum to visit us we pleaded we
were set upon by those vile cunts from Tottenham, who
picked on us the innocent to venge some deadly feud from
bygone days. The two of us got thick as tea leaves in a pot

that's stewed too long and hatched out in our white and cosy
starched beds a dozen saucy plots of murders, armed assaults
and robbery with harm, bank raids so neatly planned in dead
of night . . . of rape's delight we'd chat . . . exchange a tale or
two of cold-blood deeds we done in alleys dark as hell and
other heinous escapades too heinous to retell.

MIKE: ⎱ Yeah, that's how it happened . . . Yeah, that's it . . . she
LES: ⎰ was a bitch, a slag of advanced vile, a pint of filth . . . but
still . . .

SCENE 2

Silent Film Sequence.
Piano.
A silent film now ensues performed in the staccato, jerky motion of an
old movie. It shows MIKE *calling on* SYLV *– meeting* MUM *and* DAD *–*
going for a night out – SYLV *is attracted to* LES *– a mock fight. They*
are separated and SYLV's *long monologue comes from it. The movie*
sequence reinforces and fills in the events of scene 1.

SCENE 3

Sylv's long speech . . . She was there.

SYLV: At it they went . . . it weren't half fun at first it weren't my
fault those jesting-jousting lads should want a tournament of
hurt and crunch and blood and shriek . . . all on my dress it
went . . . That's Micky's blood I thought . . . it seemed to
shoot up from something that cracked . . . I saw him
mimicking an oilwell . . . though he'd take off many things
for a laugh this time I did not laugh so much . . . they fought
for me . . . thy blood my royal Mick wast shed for me and
never shall the suds of Persil or Daz remove that royal
emblem from that skirt that many times you gently lifted in
the Essoldo Bethnal Green. I was that monument of flesh thy
wanton hands would smash and grab, I only clocked the

other geezer Mike, and can I help if my proud tits should draw
their leery eyes to feast on them . . . and now a hate doth
sunder our strong love and never more will my soft thighs be
prised apart by his fierce knees with 'open them thou bitch
before I ram a knuckle sandwich in thy painted boat'. I miss
him true in spite of all and did not wish to see him mashed and
broken like a bloody doll . . . but now the bastard blameth me
for all and seeks vile vengeance on my pretty head . . . which if
he tries will sorely grieve my brothers Bert and George who
will not hesitate to finish off the bits that Les did leave but all
this chat of violence I hate . . . is ultra horrible to me that
thrives on love and tongue-wrenched kisses in the back of MG
Sprites with a 'stop I'm not like that!' . . . Oh just for now
which doth ensure a second date, so hold a morsel back girls
and he'll crave it all the more.

SCENE 4

MIKE *and* LES *commence* 'If You Were the Only Girl in the World'
*which covers the bringing on of the only props – a table and chairs. On
the table are toast, a teapot with steaming tea, a tureen of baked beans, a
packet of margarine – in fact the normal tea-time scene. They sit around
the table and eat. During* DAD's *long speech he eventually destroys
everything on the table in nostalgic fury. The table and contents become
a metaphor for the battle of Cable Street – his rage becomes monstrous
and gargantuan.*

Ma and Pa.
DAD: Mum?
MUM: What?
DAD: What time does *Hawaii Five-O* come on?
MUM: What time does it come on?
DAD: Yeah!
MUM: I don't know dear . . .
DAD: She doesn't know, she watches it every night, and doesn't
  know.

MUM: (*Reading*) . . . What's a proletariat?

DAD: A geezer who lassoes goats on the Siberian mountains.

MUM: In one word I mean. Six letters.

DAD: *Panorama*'s on first . . . yeah that's worth an eyeful . . . Then we can catch *Ironside*, turn over for *The Saint* and cop the last act of Schoenberg's *Moses and Aaron*.

MUM: Charlton Heston was in that.

DAD: Machinery has taken all the joy out of work . . . the worker asks for more and more money until he breaks down the economy hand in hand with the unions who are communist-dominated and make the country ripe for a takeover by the red hordes.

MUM: You haven't paid the licence.

DAD: She's a consumer on the market, that's all, not even a human being but a consumer who's analysed for what she buys and likes by a geezer offering her a questionnaire at the supermarket – makes her feel important . . . I try to educate it but 'tis like pouring wine into the proverbial leaking barrel.

MUM: Suppose they come round.

DAD: Nobody visits us any more.

MUM: They might then you'd go to court and it would be all over the *Hackney Gazette*.

DAD: You don't want to believe all that rubbish about detector vans. That's just to scare you . . . make you think that they're on your tail . . . anyway if anyone knocks on the door we can whip the telly out sharpish like and hide it in the lavatory until they're gone . . . simple . . . say . . . 'There's been a mistake . . . your radar must have been a few degrees out and picked out the hair dryer performing on her curlers.'

MUM: But anyone can knock on the door . . . you'll have to start running every time someone knocks.

DAD: When was the last time we had a visitor – especially since the lift's nearly always broken by those little black bastards who've been moving in, and who's going to climb twenty-four floors to see us except the geezer for the Christmas money – so if anyone knocks on the door it can only be one of two things – the law inquiring after Mike since they think he's just mugged some old lady for her purse, or the TV licence man – in either case I can shove it in the loo!

MUM: Mike doesn't do things like that – I won't have you uttering such dreadful libels – my son takes after me – you won't find him taking after you – he is kind to old ladies – helps them across the road on windy days.

DAD: That was only a subtle jest you hag, thou lump of foul deformity – untimely ripped from thy mother's womb – can't you take a flaming dash of humour – that I so flagrantly waste on you – eh? What then . . . what bleeding then – thank God he's not a pooftah at least already so soon – Eh . . . where would you put your face then – if he took after me the country would rise to its feet – give itself an almighty shake – and rid itself of all the fleas that are sucking it dry . . . (*Wistful*) He could have . . . Ozzie* had the right ideas – put them into uniforms – into the brown shirts – gave people an identity. Those meetings were a sight. All them flags. Then, they knew what to do – take the law into your own hands when you know it makes sense. That beautiful summer in '38 was it? – When we marched six abreast to Whitechapel – beautiful it were – healthy young British men and women – a few wooden clubs – just in case they got stroppy down there, just the thoughts of the people letting the nation know it weren't stomaching any more of it – the drums banging out a rhythm in the front and Ozzie marching at our head. We get to Aldgate – if you didn't know it was Aldgate you could smell it – and there were us few loyal English telling the world that England is for us – and those long-nosed gits, those evil-smelling greasy kikes had barricades up – you couldn't even march through England's green and pleasant, the land where Jesus set his foot – they had requisitioned Aldgate and Commercial Road – our lads, what did they do, not turn back – not be a snivelly turn-coat but let them have it. They soon scuttered back into the tailors' shops stinking of fried fish and dead foreskins – and with a bare fist, a few

*Oswald Mosley

bits of wood, we broke a skull or two that day – but Hebrew
gold had corrupted our fair law and we were outnumbered –
what could we do – the oppressed still living there under the
Semite claw sweating their balls out in those stinking sweat
shops – could only shout 'come on lads' – they had no
stomach for it, no strength. It were for them that we had to
get through. But we were outnumbered – the Christian
Soldiers could not get through this time – not then, and what
happened – I'll tell you what happened – by not getting down
Commercial Street . . . by not getting down Whitechapel –
Alie Street, Commercial Road and Cable Street, Leman
Street we opened the floodgates for the rest – the Pandora's
bleeding Box opened and the rest of the horrors poured in.
That's what happened mate. (*Suddenly*) What's the time?!
MUM: Eight o'clock.
DAD: We've missed *Crossroads*!!?!
    (*Blackout.*)

SCENE 5

The table and its contents are splattered to the floor from prior speech.
MUM *wipes it up. The five chairs now become a row in a cinema – we
see the different films by the piano suggesting the theme from a
'Weepie', a 'Western' and the characters relating to them all –* MIKE
chats up SYLV – DAD *goes to the toilet offstage – much vomiting and
noise – people change seats –* SYLV *leaves and* MIKE *follows – chat is
improvised until we see the scene with* MIKE *and* SYLV *in 'How the
Two Fought for the Possession of'. During it* DAD *and* LES *become
chorus and mates of* MIKE.

SCENE 6

How the Two Fought for the Possession of.
SYLV: She were in ingredients of flesh-pack suavely fresh . . .
    deodorized and knicker white . . . lip-gleam and teethed . . .

15

shoes thick-wedged with seam running up the back of her leg as if to point the way to tourists pruriently lost . . .

MIKE: She became with me a fun palace in which almighty raging Technicolor and panoramic skin-flicks and three-act dramas would be enacted, a veritable Butlins in one piece of equipment shaped-round-curve and press the button lights flash up . . . there's the bell and off to round one . . . 'Hallo darlin' . . . fancy thee a chat, a meal, a stroll, a drink in the Cock and Bull surrounding a Babycham or two and plethoras of witty verbiage spewing from my gutter mouth . . . with a larf or two . . . they say a laugh doth provide the key to open Pandora's Box of dirty tricks.

SYLV: Piss off thou lump. Though hast no style for me get lost . . . too old . . . too young . . . too slow . . . I'm too trim for thee and move like what you dream about (on good nights) I'm sheer unadultered pure filth each square inch a raincoat's fantasy – all there swelled full – I am the vision in your head – the fire you use to stoke your old wife's familiar stoves (you know what I mean) . . . sag not – pink tipped, tight box, plumbing perfect – switches on and off to the right touch . . . not thy thick-fingered labourer's paws thou slob and street-corner embellishment . . . thou pin-table musician . . . thy flesh would ne'er move – would shrink under my glare – so try.

MIKE: Tasty verily – so thou, bitch, seeks to distress my johnny tool with psychological war, humiliating it into surrender-shrink . . . I could mash thee into and ooze with my personality-plus once turned on . . . Full blast . . . dance thee to death and once touched, one clawful of lust-fingered-spread-squeeze resist that hot-bitch how many up and downs have thee got stacked away merrily depreciating unless thou dost invest wisely and shed a few on the market sample-like be greedy not and unleash a few.

SYLV: I wrap my goodies up for special heroes crashing thigh-clutched Harleys and angels of hell, leather skinned, tattooed in violent histories of battles too screaming delirious for verbal-mere-pub-splatter . . . loose-tongued garbage in the

vile (look-for-the-red-door) with a blah blah . . . you are
out-classed. You. You.

MIKE: I'll descend on thee like a moon probe, thou planet of
delights fleshy . . . advance my antennae, vibrating back to
the lust-computerizing cells the sanguine goodies that do lie
unmined . . . I'll chart thy surfaces until thou criest from
within thy depths, subterranean and murky and foetid
swamps, 'Mike oh Mike', fluting gurgled falsettos from thy
lips of coral, 'What dost thou dooo! . . .' I'll rip off my
clothes and gaberdine and make thee view the sight that sent
Penelope mad and wait ten years for that . . . the girth of a
Cyclops to stun to stab, screams like Attila, growls, snarls,
froths, foams and speaks to you in a thousand ways. The
length of an ass, the stamina of a Greek, the form of
Michelangelo's David, the strength of Westminster oak, as
solid as a rock, as tricky as a fox, as lithe as a snake, as
delicate as a rose, the speed of a panther, reflexes match the
piston power of the Flying Scotsman, as hot as hell – as the
forge whereby the shoes are beaten for the horses that drag
the sun round the earth each day, as pretty as Paris, its
helmet matches the battering ram that felled the walls of
Troy, its shape like the crest of Achilles, *balls* like the great
cannon that Pompeii used to subdue the barbarian, as
spherical as the mighty shield of Ulysses, as rich in goodies as
the Tiber bursting its banks, its juices as sweet as the honey
from the little wasps of Lesbos that only live a day, as sweet
as the dripping that mum puts on the Sunday joint, and with
this magic sceptre that laser-like splits and cracks through
walls, I'll fill you full till thou'll not feel one shred of space
not occupied by flesh-blood-splech-filled-slurp . . . tongue
tied, lava flow-flesh eat. Where thy arse rises creamily
mocking Bertorelli's ice-cream, the trembling domes of the
mosques of Omar bounce, weave, bob, groan and whine.
Oh, you're the spring time after fierce winter . . . buds
sprout . . . opening . . . little whisper in the hawthorn . . .
Oh! I thought thy planet shook then, caught thee then a
word did it . . . Pandora's Box teases open, does it with a yes

. . . yes . . . yes . . . No! No!
YESYESYESYESYESYESYESYESYESYES . . .
(*Blackout.*)

SCENE 7

Sylv's Longing Speech.

SYLV: I for once would like to be a fella, unwholesome both in
deed and word and lounge around one leg cocked up and car
keys tinkling on my pinky. Give a kick* at talent strolling
and impale them with an impertinent and fixed stare . . .
hand in Levi-Strauss and teeth grinding, and that super
unworrisome flesh that toys between your thighs, that we
must genuflect and kneel to, that we are beaten across the
skull with. Wish I could cruise around and pull those tarts
and slags whose hearts would break as he swiftly chews us up
and spits us out again . . . the almighty boot! Nay, not fair
that those pricks get all the fun – with their big raucous
voices and one dozen weekly fucks . . . cave mouths, shout,
burp and Guinness soaked . . . If I dare do that . . . 'What an
old scrubber-slag-head' utter their fast and vicious lips . . . so
I'd like to be a fella. Strolling down the front with the lads
and making minute and limited wars with knife-worn
splatter and invective splurge. And not have the emblem of
his scummy lust to Persil out with hectic scrub . . . just my
johnny tool to keep from harm and out of mischief . . . my
snarling beasty to water and feed from time to time to rotten
time . . . to dip my wick into any old dark and hot with no
conscience or love groan . . . doth he possess the plague in
gangrened bliss to donate to me and not give a shit. I am
snarled beneath his bristly glass-edged jaw, beneath a
moving sack of leer and hard and be a waste-bin for his
excessives and embellishments and No . . . no . . . not
tonight my friend, a dangerous time is here in case your

*eye up

18

tadpoles start a forest fire in my oven or even just a bun . . .
you won't will you? . . . you will be careful (Yes!) . . . you
won't . . . not inside (No!) Not tonight . . . ('Doth thou not
love me then') he quests ('nor feel my intense pain, then see
me not again, for you must sacrifice thy altar of lust-pink and
pornographia to my tempered sullen and purple swollen
flesh.') Oh Micky! Micky! Wait until tomorrow.
('Tomorrow I may be dead,' he chants in dirge of minor key
. . . 'by then my softly flesh may lie in shreds and curling on
the streets a victim of nuclear aggro from the powers that
deal out death on wholesale scale and liquidize your little
Mick to tar, and what was once a silken mass of moving
ecstasy programmed by filthy raunchy lust lay now a charred
and bitter heap.') Oh who can put it back again those swivel
hips/ball-bearing joints flicker spine and tongue like a
praying mantis . . . ('so listen', he adds 'dunk-head and
splatter-pull . . . seize the time before time doth seize thee
. . . you of the intricate wrist and juice imbiber from the holy
North and South.' He sprach . . . 'Give me all now or "it"
may with my balls explode, such things are known when
passion's smarting angels are defied and I may die in
loathsome sickness here upon this plastic and Formica divan
(mum and dad meanwhile in deathly lock of wrath from
heavy bingo economic loss) . . .') So wrench open deflower
unpeel, unzip . . . pull off . . . tear round knee tights stuck
. . . get your shoes off . . . Ow. Knickers (*caught on heel*) . . .
OOOh, zip hurts . . . dive in and out . . . more a whip in,
like a visit – quick, can't stay just sheltering from the rain –
cup o'tea hot and fast . . . hot plunge-squirge and sklenge
mixed for a brief 'hallo'. A rash of oohs and aaaahs quiver
and hummmmmmy . . . mmm . . . then hot and flushy he
climbs off (come in number four) and my tears those holy
relics of young love tracing mortal paths to Elysium down
my cheeks . . . while the 'he' with fag choke and smoke . . .
tooth-grin-zip-up . . . me lying looking at the future flashing
across the ceiling. He, flashing his comb through his barnet
and reddened cheeks blood soaked (like a saucy cherub, so

lovable sometimes you know how boys have this lovely thing
about them, some little-boy habit that makes them adorable,
crushable-eatable-sweetable-dolly cuddly though sometimes
you could kill them) and me lying there a pile of satiate bone
and floppy tits flesh-pinched and crack-full of his slop
containing God only knows what other infernos but thought
I tasted something very strange on his straining dangle which
he is wont to offer to me sacrificial like . . . Oh let me be a
bloke and sit back curseless, nor forever join the queue of
curlered birds outside the loo for dire-emergency . . . do we
piss more than men or something . . . nor break my heels in
escalators and flash my ass, ascending stairs, to the vile
multitude who fantasize me in their quick sex-lustred movies
in which I am cast as the queen of slut and yield . . . let me be
a bloke and wear trousers stuffed and have pectorals instead
of boobs, abdominal and latissimus-dorsi, a web of knotted
muscular armature to whip my angered fist into the flesh-
pain of sprach-offenders who dare to cast on me their leery
cautious minces . . . stab them with fear and have a dozen
flesh-hot weekly . . .sleep well and mum fussed, breakfast
shoved, 'who's been a naughty boy then', to this pasty wreck
of skin and bone gasping in his bed skiving work through
riotous folly, bloodlet assault and all night bang and 'our
lad's a lad, and sown his wild then has he and did you cut
yourself a slice' . . . while 'get yourself to the office Sylv or
you'll be late,' and the sack in its bed is parlering for another
cup of rosy. He's lying in bed whiles I'm on the
Underground getting goosed in the rush hour between Mile
End and Tottenham Court Road by some creepy asshole
with dandruff, a wife and three accidental kids and who's
probably in the accounts department . . . most perverts come
from there.

SCENE 8

LES *comes down downstage and mimes office scene, says* 'Miss Smith would you please take this to the accounts department.' *As she complies he gooses her and shrieks with maniacal joy thus fulfilling the prophecy in her last speech. His leaping up and down dissolves into a seaside scene –* MIKE *bouncing a ball.* SYLV *skipping, etc.* DAD *and* MUM *enter.*

DAD: Years ago things were good, you got value out of your money, a dollar was five bob, a summer's day was hot and sunny like a summer's day, you weren't short changed, you got your full twelve hours' worth, then we'd take the train from Liverpool Street to Leigh-on-Sea and walk to Southend, go to the Kursaal Amusements . . . (*On the words 'Kursaal Amusements' the cast become bumper cars – roller coasters. The ghost train. 'I've Got a Lovely Bunch of Coconuts' is sung – What the Butler Saw. Ice-cream sellers. The Carousel. Swimming in the sea.* MUM *gets out the sandwiches and Tizer –* SYLV *takes a photo, then so does* MIKE. *The scene should be improvised and the mime accurate and clear. The piano reinforces all the vignettes. It leaves* LES *alone on stage at the end of the last photograph. The scenes of fun at Southend delicately indicating* LES*'s sense of isolation.*)

SCENE 9

Les's Tale of Woe when he did Sup on Porridge.

LES: (*Start slow pianissimo and build*) I was lonely, you know what I mean. Just lonesome basically I think, like is one born that way, I always felt lonely as if it was something like a habit, or the colour of your hair . . . like even a bit of clobbering now and then, the taste of pain and blood, was like an act of love to me: so when two nifty lads went round the back to bundle, it could be like your bird that you pulled round for stand-up charvers. And sometimes you would pull ('cause you were lonely basically) anything that came along . . . so she looked at me, I crossed the road and gave it a bit of chat, just some bird of tender years or jail bait if you like. Maybe fourteen or fifteen. I said meet me after work, she said OK why not, with a tiny giggle and freckles leaping all over the place, and I was working in this dump, impersonating Frankenstein, a place where you stood round pretending to be busy – one of those stores where you'd try to con people into buying what they didn't want, a grimy little men's wear shop, not a geary boutique but full of rotten little grotty striped ties and collar studs, ('don't forget to dust the cuff-links Les. Straighten out the ties Les') where you stood around dying and acquiring bad breath, pop eyed for a pathetic wet customer to bleed. Horrible beige pullovers bought by the wives of Irish navvies who'd come back to change it half a dozen times 'cause we always bunged them whatever size we had in stock ('don't take a swap Les, get their gelt, they can always change it') . . . incredibly crummy blazers hanging in a rack like dead fish on parade, shirts with drab little collars with a million pins, in two-tone checks that hangmen and clerks would buy with shit-coloured ties to go with them . . . and maybe a cardigan in maroon . . . this month's colour . . . the wives trotting round the mirror anxious for their fifty bob, the manager's loathsome mask that he wears for a face creases like Fu Manchu. 'A nice tie to go with it sir? How are you fixed for shirts . . . Okayeee?' His eyes look like two gobs of phlegm, he sits in the back room where they kept those fucking horrible Y-front pants that make you look like a rupture case – he'd sit there so greasy you could fry him – in that dirty little back room he'd be watching – having his crummy little tea break . . . ''ere Les, go get us a cake will ya son . . . a chocolate éclair or something' . . . 4.15 his looked-forward-to tea break in a day that poured down boredom like yellow piss . . . his frog's eyes bulging in case you didn't sell the shop-soiled crew neck six sizes too big to some innocent black cunt. 'Yeah it fits you beeauutiful! Lovely shade, it goes with anything' . . . he spits as he rushes out of the back room like a great huge dirty spider with bits of éclair sticking

to his revolting fat lips . . . 'Fuck me! Les we got to top
yesterday's figure,' he squelched from the side of the mouth,
a hiss like a rat's fart . . . but the black is confused by being
surrounded by faces the colour of plague victims, all the
retchy salesmen with bent knees and worn-out grins. Yellow-
teethed vultures whose eyes vaguely send out a couple more
volts every time the shop door opens. 'Only take thirty
minutes for lunch on Saturday – busy day for shirts' . . .
some slag says 'that one in the window', 'Oh show me which
one you mean love', any excuse to escape and breathe some
fresh air fumes from the lorries and buses belching past
which is as fresh as a Scottish loch compared to the smell in
the shop of rotten cancered flesh laced by a few farts when
everyone scatters. 'Oh fuck, Harry's farted again' . . .
chortle-burp . . . all the macabre and twisted figures of
humanity oozed through that deceased testament to Beau
Brummel, that charnel house of gaberdine and worsted hell
. . . the living corpses – slack mouths and brains waiting for
6 p.m. or death, one of the two or both – hands in pockets
playing with anything that reminded them that they had a
tiny dot of feeling left – standing there like it was a way of
life. I was thinking of that bird which was making me very
anxious about the Hickory-Dickory and impatient to act out
a few skin scenarios floating around in my skull. At 6 p.m.
the morgue closed for the night. I'd check the gelt I half-
inched, not a bad day a few ties wrapped round my waist –
given a dozen pairs of socks to my mate and watch Mr Greasy
with fag hanging out of his perpetual mouth check his cash.
The cunt never found out 'cause his brains were soaked in
grease, his lungs in cancer and phlegm and his jacket in
dandruff . . . so I escaped from that place wondering how I
might burn it to the ground with all of them frying in the
manager's grease. I saw her as planned and she was waiting
for me like she said she would, and that had kept me going
for the day – had stopped me from going insane, the idea of
the two of us hacking away at each other's goodies – that was
something real, alive . . . that would give a bit of meaning to

my life – us two locked away in a little cosy place, where I
could crawl out of my skin and get into hers, sweat, pant and
shriek – so she was standing there, happy like it was Xmas
and she said yes and I took her back to my pad all freckling
and giggling and then she delivers her history in a funny
Irish – how she's pissed off at home with a mad Irish dad
who beats her and whiles I pacify her with a quick, svelte and
heroic in and out, she says could she stay with me since she's
bound to be clobbered by her paddy daddy for being so late.
I demur to the riotous demand with full awareness of the
Law's nastiness to the souls who taste young flesh and
instruct her to the bus to take her back to evil Kilburn. Just
one hour later I was in the middle of some shrewd
interpretations of the theory of relativity and just getting into
the quantum theory and boggling how light would take 200
billion years to get round the universe, when bang bang at
the door and two thick-eared brainless cops come yobbing
in. Dressed in the kind of clobber I'd been flogging all day,
scaring the shit out of me and the cats – the mad Irish had
gone to the johnny law with some mad tale of rape and
kidnap to avoid chastisement at the hands of dirt-head dad.
Grabbing me in their thick fingers (not made for Chopin's
'Etudes') they call me 'dirty bastard' and other unflattering
epithets while breathing their foul vomit breath in my face.
'I'll kill thee' I spray (hair on end) 'not now, not tomorrow
but one day I'll eat your eyeballs, I'll bathe you in acid, I'll
stab your fat guts with ice picks when lying in your bed
beer-soaked bloated, thick with haze and swill like drunken
pigs. I'll stab and thrust until your tripe explodes,' which
doubtless did not go down very well, since they pounded all
manner of horny fist into my soft and sweet flesh . . . those
harbingers of death . . . those wholesale legal sadists . . .
those lawmen did believe the slag, which got her off the
hook, and rendered carte of blanche to them for fun and
thump, and poor old Les before a graven magistrate is
dragged who chides and moralizes 'bout snatch too young for
me while thinking of his handicap in bed and golf and house

in Esher Surrey, his furtive weekly whore and sessions of
paid lash, looking down at me from dizzy heights he says he
would be lenient and I reply from the bottom of my black
and lying soul, of 'heartfelt sorrow', and 'never again', and
then he said, 'three years I curse on thee' and as he did I
heard my mouth reply that he would die a death in fire so
slow he'd rather be eaten alive by ants while bathed in honey
. . . 'I'll kill you a thousand times over' . . . I shouted to the
world at large and as they dragged me screaming down some
cold stone corridor my shouts sent curses ripping through his
skull, and now my curse comes true.

MIKE: So how did you kill him Les?

LES: I doubt if I should let on now, lest hungry ears attend, you
do not know whose flappy lugs may bring a fate too horrible
for verbs upon my lovely head. But content yourself I did.

MIKE: There's no one here but us and our rabid desires.

LES: I think I hear the beating of a hundred hearts.

MIKE: Only us and our imaginations, as foul as Vulcan's stithy.

LES: What are those sighs and murmurs, soft groans?

MIKE: The punters who paid for a seat to witness thy foul and
cruel beauty, that will haunt them in their dreams.

LES: Do you mean we're in a play?

MIKE: Something of that kind.

LES: I am not, even if you may be.

MIKE: You mean to say . . .

LES: Exactly, you sussed it true, I am no player who struts and
frets his hour upon the stage and then is heard no more.

MIKE: You guessed aright, I am that merry wanderer of the night.

LES: You've made a time slip into the wrong play.

MIKE: I am caught in a time-space trajectory.

LES: Can you see me . . . I can only just see you.

MIKE: Yes, but you're fading fast. What's happening?

LES: Think you've hooked on to an errant radio wave from C56,
your own waves are sacrificing themselves to its force until
your anti-matter coalesces.

MIKE: Fuck! What can I do . . .

LES: Nothing, just go with it. I'll tell your mum and Sylv.

MIKE: OK. See ya around sometime . . . I've lost you now . . .
can you hear me? . . .

LES: Only just . . . see ya . . .

(*The whole cast become involved in the latter part of the scene
. . . floating slowly in space until* MUM *settles down with legs
comfortably sprawled over* DAD *on two chairs stage left. The
three other actors face offstage and* MUM *is lit in her own space.
She takes out a cigarette and commences her speech.*)

SCENE 10

Mum's Point of View.
DAD *is sleeping.*

MUM: Sometimes I get gorged in my throat I see him sleeping –
lump sweaty, beer gutted – farty – no hope – thick brained
and me the other half of nothing fed with electric media swill
– consumer me – *Hawaii Five-O* – *Z Cars* – *Coronation Street*
– *Beat the Clock* – *University Challenge* – *Sunday Night at the
London Palladium* – *On the Buses* – *Play of the Month* – *Play
of the Week* – *Watch With Mother* – tea, fags – light and bitter
– ha! ha! and ho! ho! Bingo – Eyes down – clickety click –
What the Papers Say – Reg Varney – *The Golden Shot* – Live
Letters – Tits – Green Shield Stamps (*Pause.*) Hallo dear
how are you? Turn over shut up and let me sleep – fart belch
the music of the spheres. Got a clean shirt? Who's running at
Epsom? 500 more troops being flown in tonight – the Pill is
safe – abortions rise – I would like to practise today –
Tippett's 'Sonata number 3'; six hours of it, I must be ready
for my BBC recital on Wednesday – then I may pair it with
Mozart's 'Concerto in C' – Terry Riley, mind you, needs
dextrous finger work – I'll leave that for now and pick up my
percolator at the Green Shield shop – Wall's pork sausages
for supper and Fray Bentos peas – McDougall's flour for a
smooth pastry – do I smell? Does my mouth taste like an
ashtray? Will my lover meet me after I play Brünnhilde in
'The Ring' at the stage door to Covent Garden and buy me

filet mignon in Rules Café or the Savoy? Will we drink
champagne and discuss our next production of Verdi's
Otello? He's longing to play Otello – but wants Bernstein to
direct – I'd be happy with Visconti really – Maria is coming
to tea – must get some Lyons jam tarts – I met Hemingway in
the Brasserie Lipp today, he said my poetry soars to heaven.
Come and have some wine with Gertrude, there will be some
very nice people there.

FATHER: (*Waking up*) Shut your gob. Can't ya let me bleeding
    sleep?
    (*Blackout.*)

SCENE 11

Mike and Les.

MIKE: How's Doris – the imbiber of thy resin with her holy
    North and South?

LES: All right.

MIKE: Seeing her tonight?

LES: No!

MIKE: Oh! What happened?

LES: Loaded off her box to other's greedy paws.

MIKE: Almighty slag.

LES: I told her to get to a nunnery, in other words piss off.

MIKE: I thought you were a bit touchy.
    (*Pause.*)

LES: I was on the bus today – I jumped on the 38 goin' towards
    Balls Pond Road, the one that goes to Leyton – I mounted at
    Holborn – just been to the British Museum to look at the
    Elgin Marbles which were double fair but too big to half-inch
    and I was standing, since there were no seats, in the recess
    where the clippie normally stands – you know when it's quiet
    she stands there chattin' and making thin jokes to the seats
    that face each other, having a quiet fart as the bus makes its
    last journey down Piccadilly up Shaftesbury Avenue you
    know past *Jesus Christ* – up Charing Cross passed that

cinema showing *I was A Go Go Dancer in a Saigon Brothel* – spins around the Centre Point Synagogue and skates down Holborn – up Mount Pleasant Post Office where the spade post office workers are skiving in the betting shop, past the Angel where Joe Lyons used to be, where one's mum supped famous cups of rosy amidst merry parlance, now it's boarded up, down Essex Road, past Collins Music Hall, now a rotten wood yard, past Alfredo's café, you know where one gets great toasted liver sandwiches, streaks past the ABC, now a shitty bingo hall to the end of Essex Road, now a casbah full of shishkebab.

MIKE: A veritable tour of our golden city.

LES: Shall I continue?

MIKE: Pray do.

LES: Anyway I jumped on at Holborn and stood in that recess where the clippie stands, when I saw the most awful cracker. A right darlin' – I stood there clocking it, wanting her to get the message, dulcet filthed, she was blonde with medium-length hair, dyed straw but soft and straight and her legs phenomenal. She had this short skirt on – and it had tucked gently between her legs in case she flashed her magic snare to some snatch bandit like me – and faces jumped on and off never quite hiding my angel from me but those legs with well-carved calves poured into some very high thick-wedged shoes. She was a darlin' – I could have breakfasted out of her knickers so sweetly pure she was – I could have drunk the golden nectar from that fountain, I could have loved her – wrapped her legs round my throat, her bright arse trembling in my hands. Divine she was and wore dark glasses but not so dark I couldn't see that finest glint as she occasionally clocked me vardering her like an ogre with a hard-on, ready to leap across the bus and say darlin' climb aboard this, but she was almost too perfect. I stood all the way – unable to leave, like a sentinel at the post and my lover was there – and I thought, Mike, I thought of Doris and I thought of all the fat scrubbers I get with soggy tits – I thought of all those dirty scrubbers and how, just once in my life I'd like to walk down the street with that. Why don't we chat up classy snatch? Why is it that we pull slags? We pull what we think we are Mike – it tumbled then – it dropped – the dirty penny – that we get what we ARE. What we think we are, so when we have a right and merry laugh with some unsavoury bunk-up or gang bang behind the Essoldo we are doing it to ourselves. We are giving ourselves what we deserve. It came to me then – here it was, the most delectable snatch in the world REAL with those INCREDIBLE pins and CLEAN – and then she stirred just ever so little it was but she knew I was lapping it up – and she uncrossed her legs to get up. She was going but maybe my wires got through to her and she thought why not give that geezer – he's not a bad looking bloke – a flash and as she uncrossed her DIVINE THIGHS I swivelled my sockets up there and some creep moved right in front of her but I just caught the slightest glimpse of heaven – the clouds passed over the sun but it reappeared again – she stood up on the platform waiting to leap off at Farringdon Road with that thin skirt on – a thin black cotton skirt – God she must have known that the sun pours through that skirt – no slip, just her AMAZING FUCKING FORM. Up to the ARSE. Like she was naked, standing there waiting for the bus to stop at Mount Pleasant where she jumped off – and I wanted to jump off Mike – I wanted to get off the bus and run after her – but what could I say – she strode down the street – strong on these DELIRIOUS PEGS with those nasty post office workers leering her beautiful form with their dim and faded jellies and I couldn't get off the bus – I didn't have the guts – I didn't know what to say to her Mike! What words could my gob sprach?! And then I saw her cross into Clerkenwell Road when she disappeared.

MIKE: 38 bus! You want to get yourself a motorbike.

SCENE 12

The two lads wander upstage to a special spot – MIKE *turns* LES *into a motorbike and jumps on his back using* LES's *arms as handlebars. The two clearly create the sound of a motorbike revving up and changing gear during the scene. The strength of the engine and the movement as it careers round corners should be apparent.*

Oh for Adventures.

MIKE: I am a Harley Davidson with ape-hangers or maybe I am a chopper made to measure to fit me – a built-in Triumph 5000 cc. Perhaps I am a Harley Davidson with high-rise bars. A Yamaha or a Suzuki 1500 cc. Yeah, but who wouldn't mind a Vincent HRD 10,000 cc.

LES: With apes?

MIKE: No – not on your Vincent HRD it's too classy, not on that – that's sacrilege. At a 150 a ton and a half of sublime speed tearing gut winded flailing flesh pulled – your glasses stabbing in your eyes – ice ripping off your face – the vibrations pulsating through each square inch of skin between your thighs power lies – at 2000 cc my throttle-twist grip lightly, oh so delicately held – not too much rev! We skate! We fly! Between my thighs I grip her tight – she won't budge – won't skid – road clears for us – it opens up like a river – the cars farting families in VWs and Fords, with dogs and kids smearing up the rear windows and granny spouting they ought to be exterminated – standing still they seem – I streak past the ponces and hairdressers in Minis, Sprites, MGs, menswear salesmen in green Cortinas, or ancient Cadillacs driven by ageing movie stars cruising for rough trade and liking the leather-loin boys with long records of glorious GBH tattooed on the helmets of their cocks. I slow down to 150 miles an hour and chat it up – her face is hanging off her skull, she sees what grows between my knees and creams her jeans. 'Stop James,' she says and we split – down to Joe's café at the intersection where the M1 sludges reluctantly off into Luton, I mean who wouldn't be – there

behind the café behind the pantechnicons and articulated
lorries I ram it into her ancient North and South. 'Take out
your teeth you old slag,' and I leave her with a happy grin on
her toothless retchy boat. James carries her off with a nod
suggesting here we go again – never mind it's all in a day's
work – start up my beauty once more nice and gently – open
up the throttle very slightly, no more than an eighth, depress
the kick starter – now I feel it coming to life – warming,
buzzing down there it's loving it – she's randy now. Now
kick the starter in the jacksie – smash the brute down –
ZAPP! We're off – she rises – she moves like it had teeth –
like it was hungry – like it KNEW where to go and she sings
to me everything's checked, everything's beautiful all
checked.

LES	MIKE
Headlamp?	Check
Tail-lamp?	Check
Pilot bell?	Check
Carburettor?	Check
Alter-jet needle?	Right
Position?	Right
Float chamber?	Right
Tickler?	Right
Sparking plugs?	Check
Clean out?	Right
Oil your lubricator?	Lovely
Remove dynamo?	Lovely
Inspect brush gear?	Lovely
Keep it jacked up?	Lovely
Ready to start?	Lovely
How's your oil?	Lovely
Stand astride	Yeah!
Turn on the taps	Yeah!
Open your throttle	Yeah!

Song

> I am a Harley Davidson
> I am a Harley Davidson
> I am a Vincent HRD
> I am a Vincent HRD
> I fly like a king
> I kill like a sting
> I smash down the road
> I crush those other fuckers
> Those Hell's Angels like toads

MIKE: ⎫
LES: ⎭ (*Sing* 'Underneath the Arches'.)

(*The two boys separate and become a raging duet enacting their passion for the bike. At the end of the song which is screamed out they go into* 'Underneath the Arches', *sung delicately, which covers the next dining scene and the table is brought on in the condition it went off –* DAD *repeating the first part of the speech again.*)

SCENE 13

Dad's Soliloquy for Happier Days.

DAD: Years ago things were good, you got value out of your money, a dollar was five bob, a summer's day was hot and sunny like a summer's day – you weren't short changed, you got your full twelve hours' worth, then we take the train from Liverpool Street to Leigh-on-Sea and walk to Southend, go to the Kursaal Amusements. It was fun then. On Sunday you'd get cockles and whelks from Tubby Isaacs on the corner of Goulston Street, eat them outside and walk down Wentworth Street to the station past the warehouses – 'Got the sandwiches mum?' – 'Yeah – all packed' – bottle of Tizer – your Mike only five then before he saw the inside of a detention centre or Borstal. That was his bad environment that was – all those dirty rough-necked Irish bog-diggers whose kids set him up to snatch handbags – never got it from me . . . Never mind. Then we jump on the train – mum and Ethel, her sister – she don't half gas but what a larf . . .

MIKE: Who's Ethel?

DAD: You know. Big fat Ethel, covered in warts. No disrespect but she looked like a tree trunk coming down the road.

LES: She suffered from tree trunk legs.

DAD: Elephantiasis is the correct medical name. I looked it up. Here, young Mike was a terror even then. Unscrewing the light bulbs and chucking them out of the window.

MIKE: (*Proud*) I did that?

DAD: Of course you did, all the way down to Southend. (*Bop bop bopbop*)

MIKE: I never.

DAD: You did, five years old you were. You stood on my shoulders! I still have the bill in the sideboard from Eastern Region. They banned us in the end . . . we'd go up to the station and say five please . . . they'd say piss off out of it! . . . no more light bulbs! You remember, we became known as no more light bulbs! Weren't we, mum?

MUM: (*Distant manner*) What? . . .

DAD: Never mind. The East End was rough then, still half down, and the kids would catch the water skaters from those septic rancid tanks near the bomb sites. All the abes used to sit outside in Anthony Street 'cause they liked a natter and would you believe it – they had the nerve to open a theatre where you had to understand Yiddish – what a gall! Many a time I'd been over there for a quiet afternoon kip, paid my one and six and they'd say, 'You understand Yiddish?' I'd say what you mean 'Yiddish' and they'd say piss off out of it!

LES: In the middle of London.

MIKE: It's not like a language . . . it's like a code.

DAD: You're right son . . . it's a bloody secret code.

SYLV: Do you know any dad?

DAD: Of course I do . . . I do know a bit . . . I went to night school.

SYLV: Say something then.

DAD: Let's see . . . turn the cogs back a bit . . . uum . . . 'My life!' That's Yiddish, that's four thousand years old that phrase.

LES: Sounds English to me.

DAD: Of course it's not bloody English . . . it's four thousand years old . . . that stems from the heart of Yiddisher land . . . it's been fooling the bloody Arabs for years that phrase . . . walking down Jerusalem high street they're all going, 'My life, my life'. They haven't a bloody clue . . . they think it means something else . . . they think it means the tanks are coming. Of course it doesn't!

LES: What's it mean?

DAD: What's it mean?

LES: Yeah.

DAD: I'll tell you what it means . . . My life actually means . . . My life!

LES: What's bloody secret about that?

DAD: I'm glad you asked that. You think that because it's a foreign language it's a foreign code . . . but it's not . . . that's the whole point . . . you get it! (*Pushes* LES *over*.) You dumb shmuck. Anyway, we'd go on the train on that hot Sunday morning, music playing in Liverpool Street Station (still do that do they?) (*Sings 'We'll Meet Again' in falsetto*.) Vera Lynn. Magnificent woman.

LES: Yeah.

MIKE: She's dead ain't she?

SYLV: She's not dead.

DAD: Of course she's not dead . . . don't be so insulting! She's ninety-six years old, but she's not dead . . . she looks like she's dead . . . she sings like she's dead . . . but she's not dead . . . I went to school with her.

SYLV: You were at school with her?

DAD: I was at school in the same class . . . we were very close friends.

MUM: But you ain't ninety-six.

DAD: Of course I'm not ninety-six you stupid bonehead.

MUM: Well how could you be in the same class?

DAD: She was a slow learner . . . she didn't start her schooling till forty-three on account of disease . . . very backward . . . she used to sing all the time . . . what do you mean sending her up! She's done more for her country than you have. She's served in four bloody world wars she has. At the bloody front serving . . . what do you know about it you bloody raging suppurating faggot?

LES: (*Faggoty*) I don't know what you mean.

DAD: She was honoured by our great and glorious Queen. She went down to Buck House last week in our great and glorious Jubilee year . . . ninety-six years old . . . knelt before the Queen . . . she's not just bleeding old boring Vera from Bethnal Green any more . . .

MIKE: Oh, what's she now?

DAD: (*Authoritatively*) Sir Vera! (*Laughter*) You fell for that one . . . well it's true. Anyway, Sunday morning Vera singing in Liverpool Street Station, past Hackney and then head up for the coast – what a larf we had then – candy floss, the train out to the end of the pier singing 'Roll out the barrel, we'll have a barrel of fun', listen to that!! Sung to the rhythm of the train 'We'll have a barrel of fun' – wholesome stuff know ya? – never knew what the pox was in those days – didn't exist except on the blacks and no one got near them or on a few scabby Chinese off the boats in the West India Dock road. A pack of Woodbines was a shilling and a pint was tenpence ha'penny.

MUM: (*from the distance*) Ninepence.

DAD: The oracle has spoken . . . what she say?

SYLV: Ninepence.

DAD: Ninepence! Ninepence! . . . She's right! She's right! I tell a lie it was ninepence. Doris was all right in those days. She weren't fallen apart with all that grease – makes you sick. I wonder why women become such old cart horses after they marry – after Mike came her tits dropped so low they could be seen dangling at the end of her mini skirt which she never should have worn – a mini at fifty! And all she's got in her box is a space – you could climb in her for a quiet snooze like the other night . . .

SCENE 14

Scene of the Two in Bed.
MUM: Fred. (*Pause.*)
DAD: WHAT? (*Pause.*)
MUM: Are you fucking me? (*Pause.*)
DAD: (*Dry*) No.
MUM: Yes you are – I can hear you!
    (*Blackout.*)

SCENE 15

Mum's Lament.
MUM: He's a dirty bastard at his age. If he comes home pissed out
    of his head he grabs me and calls me his doll – I'm used to
    being left alone now – get no sensation no more – years of
    neglect have taken away the edge – so when he starts on me
    it's like being assaulted, it's dirty. We always keep our
    underwear on – in bed – just his horribly belchy breath –
    once he belched in my mouth as he was giving me a reeky
    kiss – I slapped him so hard he let out an enormous fart –
    that made me so cross I slapped him again and he pissed the
    bed laughing – we haven't kissed since then. I could still do it
    I've no doubt, just the desire's faded – I almost did once –
    have an affair – a short one – I was in the Poplar Cinema –
    just past the Troxy off Commercial Road, it's now been
    condemned I think – watching Anna Neagle in that beautiful
    film *Spring in Park Lane*. Some geezer started to fiddle with
    my skirt and then touched my suspenders. I was about to
    speak my mouthpiece when I thought 'Shut up Doris behave
    like a bloke' – dirty like – so I did. His hand was very slowly
    lifting my skirt up – so slowly like he was afraid that at any
    second he'd feel an axe come down on it – go on boy I
    thought, and he was only a kid – fuck me, just a sweet kid of
    sixteen or seventeen – couldn't see me in the dark and I
    didn't like to look – shy like. So he took my hand rather

boldly I thought – and placed it on his chopper; cheeky! . . . and he had a beautiful silky hot one, all ready primed and juicy – I was getting ever so flushy and each time the usherette went past we'd freeze like two statues – I kept on pumping away – he'd be fumbling with my cami, my cami-knickers that is, and then it shot out all over the back of the next seat, whoosh!

(DAD *in the front seat reacts as if the great whoosh of sperm had landed on his head – he says, 'Was sat!?' looks up as if something has landed on him from the balcony and goes offstage mumbling things to himself like 'Something seems to be leaking out of my head.'* MUM *then continues her speech.*)

The film had just ended – Anna Neagle was just making up with Michael Wilding, and he was wiping his spunk off the front seat, not Michael Wilding, this boy next to me. When the lights come on – Oh dear – I did turn queer when I saw our Mike – dirty bugger – takes after his dad – I copped him out when he got home.

SCENE 16

Les's Speech: A Night Out.

LES: I fancy going down the Lyceum tonight. I double fancy that. (*The Lyceum music starts and* LES *and* MIKE *dance with invisible partners.* DAD *and* MUM *come on and dance in their own style –* SYLV *enters* MIKE *asks her to dance – the Andrews Sisters is played on a tape. The dancing of* MIKE *and* LES *is stylish '55 Lyceum style. A bar is created (*MUM *becomes barmaid.) Much drinking goes on. A fight nearly starts. Everyone leaves – then the two boys re-enter at a run, hit the centre spot, the music stops and the scene continues as before.*)

Being as it's Sunday we'll have Mr Ted Heath the famous band leader, not the acid bath murderer or notorious political impersonator cum weekend transvestite – and Dicky Valentine in a blue gabardine, button two, flap pockets, hip-length whistle and flute. I'll wear a roll-away collar, a Johnny Ray collar, that sails out of your neck and a skinny tie – a slim Jim. French cuffs on a trouser with a fifteen-inch bottom. What about the handsome Doneal tweed with DB lapels? Button one, patch pockets, dropped loops, cross pockets on the trousers, satin lined, eighteen-inch slip up the arse on the jacket, skirted waist. What that one? Er– yeah – it's beautiful – fingertip length velvet collar, plenty of pad in the chest ('Come on Morry, I said, more padding'). Of course when we were geary we pulled – not all slags neither, but you need wheels – no point in pulling without wheels – or you'd end up taking some scrubber down Edmonton and walking all the way back to Commercial Road at three in the morning with as often as not nothing to show for it except a J. Arthur reluctantly given at the point of a seven-inch honed and sharpened shiv menacing her jugular. When we got our wheels we pulled handsomely a much better quality of cunt. There was not much good quality cunt about then. And most of it were from Billingsgate.

(LES *exits leaving* MIKE *in his spot*.)

SCENE 17

Mike's Cunt Speech.

MIKE: I disagree with Les. We always found good cunt at the Lyceum. Friendly cunt, clean cunt, spare cunt, jeans and knicker stuffed full of nice juicy hairy cunt, handfuls of cunt, palmful grabbing the cunt by the stem, or the root – infantile memories of cunt – backrow slides – slithery oily cunt, the cunt that breathes – the cunt that's neatly wrapped in cotton, in silk, in nylon, that announces, that speaks or thrusts, that winks that's squeezed in a triangle of furtive cloth backed by an arse that's creamy springy billowy cushiony tight, knicker lined, knicker skinned, circumscribed by flowers and cotton, by views, clinging knicker, juice ridden knicker, hot knicker, wet knicker, swelling vulva knicker, witty cunt, teeth smiling the eyes biting cunt, cultured cunt, culture

vulture cunt, finger biting cunt, cunt that pours, cunt that
spreads itself over your soft lips, that attacks, cunt that
imagines – cunt you dream about, cunt you create as a
Melba, a meringue with smooth sides – remembered from
school boys' smelly first cunt, first foreign cunt, amazing
cunt – cunt that's cruel. Cunt that protects itself and makes
you want it even more cunt – cunt that smells of the air, of
the earth, of bakeries, of old apples, of figs, of sweat of hands
of sour yeast of fresh fish cunt. So – are we going Les? We
might pick up a bit of crumpet.

SCENE 18

At the end of the last speech the two boys return to the chairs – MIKE
*starts slowly to speak the song 'Daisy, Daisy Give Me Your Answer
Do' acting it out to* SYLV *who reacts favourably eventually. They all
join in until it becomes a fracas – at the peak of the noise when all are
jumping up and down and shouting –* MIKE *leaves the group –
followed by* LES *– they share the next speech – remaining in the same
two areas they opened the play with.*

SCENE 19

Resolution.
MIKE *and* LES. (*The lines can be split or spoken together, as suits the
actors.*)
     I'm sick of my house,
     I'm sick of my family –
     In fact they make me sick.
     I don't mind
     One day like the brothers Kray
     Like Reg,
     We'll be flying along happily –
     A chopper in one hand
     A dagger in my flute,

We'll see the boys in Dean Street
(''Allo son, I'll have a hundred suits').
The East End's my manor,
I mean that's what we know
Trolling down the Green
Bethnal to you –
Going down the Lye –
The Lyceum Strand –
Kicking Cypriot berks to death
With Johnny and the gang –
Where's Big Harry gone? and Curly King?
Where's hard Arthur? Where's all the hard men?
Where have they been?
We'll open a porn shop,
A knocking shop too –
We'll spring the Krays, handsome –
The Richardsons too.
We'll threaten and murder,
Connive and rob,
The law's on our side –
We'll pay the slobs.
We'll get our piece –
We'll protect their bit of trade,
The hard porn and tit shows
They'll give us our pay
Every week.
We'll eat at Mario's where the hairdressers go
We'll get fat, we'll kill and we'll knife
I hate all you pseudo bastards,
I hate you with my life.

SYLV's *Speech of Resolution*.
We will not end our days
In grey born blight – and stomp
Our hours away in fag end waste.
And kiss the minutes till they budge
While we toil in some stinking

factory – But what's the future lads
for us – where were the stars when we
were born that ordained that our birth
and death should be stamped out like
jelly babies in a jar to be sucked out
and chewed, then spat out at the end to
croak away before a flickering light
– and fill in forms at dole queues and
stand behind the sacks of skin that are called
men and women, translated into numbers
crushed in endless files – we will not end
our days like this – waiting, while ma and pa
make little noughts and crosses upon
coupons called hope-or-death – we will not
end our days like this.

MIKE: Bung us a snout. Les?

LES: OK Mike. I'll donate to thee a snout.

MIKE:
LES: } Now you know our names.

GLOSSARY OF SLANG

berk (Berkeley Hunt)	female pudenda
boat or boat race	face
bundle	fight
charver	sexual intercourse
china	friend
chopper	axe or penis
clobber	clothes
clock	pointedly look at
curly king	East End tearaway
double strong	keenly
flute	suit
give a kick	eye up
hickory dickory	time
J. Arthur (Rank)	wank
jellies	eyes
knuckle-sandwich	fist
Kray twins	East End murderers serving life
Lyceum	centre for hard tearaways in the late fifties. Formerly the theatre where Henry Irving played.
minces	eyes
mucker	friend
north and south	mouth
pegs	legs
pins	legs
pull	pick up
Richardsons	South London murderers serving life
snatch	female pudenda
snout	cigarette
sprach	speak
talent	good-looking bird
vardering	looking (early sixties gay vernacular)

WEST

or

WELCOME TO DALSTON JUNCTION

CHARACTERS

RALPH
MIKE
KEN
SYLV
LES
SID
PEARL
STEVE
MESSENGER

AUTHOR'S NOTE

West was first performed at the Donmar Warehouse, Covent Garden, in May 1983. That was its world première, although I believe a version was performed in Wagga Wagga, Australia, three years before, in 1980. But they had tampered with the text and even included a scene from *East*, thus disqualifying themselves from being the first to present *West*. *East*, my play about the East End from a young hero's point of view, was the first of a series which, naturally, inspired *West*. The BBC actually commissioned it and then found it not quite dull enough for television – much to my delight, as I was then able to stage it at a later date. Limehouse Productions and Ian Albery sponsored its first showing in London, and Limehouse have filmed it for television at the time of writing, so I hope that as *West* played before its thousands, it will soon play before its millions.

West is about courage: the courage to live according to your spirit and not the guidelines laid down for you by others, to be true to yourself, which may involve alienating others, but your truth is worth pursuing since it defines who you are. It shapes, forges and hones you into something that is not vague but clear-cut and definite. Mike's truth is to live for simple principles and to put his courage where his mouth is. He defeats the Hoxton monster and will continue to fight monsters so that others can rest safe in their beds. While the play is an allegory about demons we must defeat, it is also about an area of time and space called London and, specifically, Stamford Hill or Hackney, N16. You wore tailored suits and strutted your gear at the Lyceum, Strand, on Sunday nights. Movements were short, percussive and cool – Oscar Rabin led the band, Lita Rosa sang and the Kray twins would stand and survey their domain. I never saw them dance. Stamford Hill stood at the crossroads of Tottenham, Dalston and Hoxton and was subject to attacking forays from many directions. Such skirmishes were few, but I remember when, instead of sending a gang each time, Tottenham would send, symbolically, one of their toughest fighters to come and spread terror and challenge our leader. There was one young man from Stamford Hill who somehow elected himself to take on each one, and he did in fact beat them all. He was a frightening cur who actually put his fist through doors for practice. His name was Harry Lee. Mike is not based on a hero but is an amalgam of feelings that I had at the time and my observations of the environment.

West was first performed on 2 May 1983 at the Donmar Warehouse, London, presented by Omega Stage Ltd and Limehouse Productions Ltd. The cast was as follows:

RALPH	Ralph Brown
MIKE	Rory Edwards
KEN	Ken Sharrock
SYLV, Mike's bird	Susan Kyd
LES	Bruce Payne
SID, Mike's dad	John Joyce
PEARL, Mike's mum	Stella Tanner
STEVE	Steve Dixon
MESSENGER	Garry Freer

The HOXTON MOB are played by the same actors as Mike's gang with some subtle changes, i.e. cloth caps and chokers.

Director	Steven Berkoff
Designer	Nadine Baylis
Music	Mark Glentworth

A television production of *West* was broadcast by Channel 4 Television on 14 November 1984.

ACT ONE

Pub sequence. The stage is bare but for a line of chairs upstage whereby the cast act as a chorus for the events that are spoken, mimed and acted. A piano just offstage creates moods, adds tension and introduces themes. The piano starts up and the cast sing as the lights come up. They sing cockney songs out of order – 'My Old Man', 'I'm Forever Blowing Bubbles', 'Roll out the Barrel', 'You are my Sunshine'. LES *joins in. Time is called. They exit from the pub, leaving the boys and* SYLV. *The* GANG *explodes on to the stage and freezes.*

LES: Breathless, I was aghast when I saw / standing between the full moon and the blinking lamplight, this geezer / all armed, a certain aim he took / and felled the swarthy git from Hoxton with a deft and subtle chop / I never witnessed Mike I swear such venom and gross form in leather stacked / his coat stitched and embellished with fine lattice work of studs (to be more deadly when swung) no other weapon being handy like.

MIKE: Armed you say?

RALPH: From top to toe.

STEVE: From head to foot.

MIKE: Then you saw not his face?

KEN: He wore his titfer up.

MIKE: By Christ, would I had been there.

LES: He would have much amazed you.

MIKE: Very like, very like.

LES: His face / his rotten grizzly boat looked like a planet that'd been boiled in nuclear wars or struck by meteors / razed by hurricanes, criss-crossed by deep canals and rank defiles / those scars were mute but telling witnesses of battles fought with weapons / grim with deadly promise / and fought to bitter ends before the shout of 'Hold, hold enough!'

RALPH: No shout of 'hold' was uttered then / not when he earned those lines / the tailor that did redistribute his face served his apprenticeship in Smithfield's bloody stalls / had habit of a thrust and chop to fell a bull and by the likes of this man's deadly cheeks / was put to death / no waiting time allowed / they fought until the streets were strewn in blood and bits of human flesh did gladden many hearts of sewer rats that night / or so I heard.

MIKE: He must be a right ugly bastard!

KEN: The face doth resemble the asshole of an elephant.

MIKE: A face like that won't launch a thousand ships or pull the scrubbers to their beds in Edmonton / Gants Hill / or Waltham Cross / so let him have his scars / his medals that he flaunts to all / to put the shits up any villain that doth take a fancy to him / for a bout of bundle round the back. That don't go down with me / you hear / you scum, impressionable as the tides that lick on any shore and gather up the muck and floating rubbers from some hectic night that others have / you who feed upon the blood that others shed / and wipe the bums of hard-faced villains / living by their very farts that you gulp down / and think you are so favoured to be near / that don't go down with me you chorus that exaggerate some slimy punk / as big in your esteem as you are small / when seen through normal eyes and not those / bent with envy / and weighted down with fear / would seem a normal sort of bloke / a fraction harder than the most at most / but not a raving Cyclops crossed with Hitler and Goliath thrown in as well / so pack up all this natter / and confess the utter wholesome gen [*truth*] you fancy not my chances with this Kong?

RON: Of course we doth, my dearest lovely Michael.
    (*They walk on the spot.*)

LES: We were only uttering the like of what we saw / destruction of the King of Hoxton's hardy pack / you know that gruesome mob / they're hard men Mike / as tough as hobnail boots / from days and nights of doing bird and eating porridge within the flinty walls of Pentonville.

KEN: And Brixton.

STEVE: Scholars of notorious hatchet men of Broadmoor / served their apprenticeships at double time in Parkhurst, Isle of Wight, 'neath the twins / who taught them ultra-subtle ways with carving knives.

RALPH: They're brought up hard / since snot-nose kids they never knew / the softer life / electric blankets when you're snug at night from pulling scrubbers / from the Locarno Streatham / or the Ly / that cold walk back to home and hearth / a glass of Tizer in the fridge and mum's left chicken soup for you to nosh.

STEVE: A bagel warming in the stove.

RALPH: Those dulcet ways doth soften us Hackney lads.

KEN: Sure we'd be good for bang with gang upon a bird / or the occasional toe to toe with hard-faced Arthur or blond tyke / from Tottenham / I've seen you fell the best / but those from Hoxton / they're not human Mike.

LES: They feel no pain / they don't wear coats in winter even.

KEN: Not to spoil their whistles / crush their shoulder pads / they don't even like pulling talent / lest they disembark their energy they wish to save / for making love to violence.

MIKE: So that's why all those tarts and slags come running to us panting / drawers at half-mast when they see a lad from Hackney or from Stamford Hill.

LES: (*Walking downstage*) Of course / their blokes just given them clobberings / and pints of crummy bitter / if they're lucky / and a game of darts / a kicking if they get in front of Arsenal v. Spurs on telly on a Saturday / their day of rest from hauling bricks around the sites, to harden gnarled hands to bunch into thick mitts or knuckle sandwiches / to finish off a pleasant evening at the Royal, Tottenham / they're not for you / I know you're hard my royal Mike – the King of Stamford Hill / I've seen you put your dukes through wooden shit-house doors for practice.

RALPH: But those hands were made for better things / like dealing royal flush and trump beneath the deck.

ALL: Right!

RALPH: Unhooking bras one-handed / whilst the other like a

subtle snake seeks other pastures.

ALL: Right!

RALPH: Or making rude and gamey gestures from fast cars at thick-brained yobs from Romford / who in slow and worn-out bangers / can only yelp and scream vile insults lashed in hate / about the nature of our origin / and flash their rotten teeth / as we slide past in fast Cortinas.

KEN: Birds galore in black / squashed in and squeaking / flapping in their awesome glee at your horsepower man.

LES: So let's forget the bundle / let's scout out what muff walks lonesome streets tonight / and drag them back to forty watts of Eric Clapton or Queen.

MIKE: Swallow it, you mean! And wear a hideous yellow on my back / to strut before a wanton ambling nymph / that's what you see for me / Mike the King of N16 / I'll drown more villains than a mermaid could / deceive more slyly than old Shylock would / and set the murderous Hoxton King to school / can I do this and cannot get his crown / balls, were he Al Capone I'd pluck it down / now listen men of little faith / beneath my gabardine and / poplin shirts / beneath my Crombie satin-lined with slanting pockets / there beats a heart of steel and will of iron / I'll crack open his skull / with this / I do a thousand press-ups every day and forearm curls / a score of chin-ups on the bar / have made my arms a vice to crush a bear / bench-press 300 pounds / those triceps aren't just ornaments you feel / 500 squats a day with poundage on my back of two grown men / have made my thighs the girth of oaks / and five score pull-ups on an inclined bench have carved a marble sculpture on my gut / feel / go on punch and break your fist on me you snively worms / just 'cause my mum fed me with bagels / cream cheese and rich bortsch you think I am a powder puff or soggy stuff thus to be shaped to humping ladies' underwear round retailers or flogging stockings out of suitcases in Oxford Street or doing knowledge on a moped with a dream of owning one fat stinking taxi cab / and sit spine-warped with 30p upon the clock / where to sir? To some ponce who vomits in the back /

or has a quick charver . . . no boy / that's not for me.

LES: Our mind's made up.

STEVE: Yeah / let him come / we'll show them what we're made of.

MIKE: That's the way. I see you now / straining like greyhounds in the slips at Harringay / let's away / arm yourselves my boys / the heat is on / those that do not fight with us this day will think themselves accursed / they were not here / get chains and mallets / choppers and fine steel / we'll give those evil bastards something to feel / we'll wrap a warning round their skulls / and they'll not bestride our streets no more / their ugly mugs scaring the police horses / causing our pregnant ladies to abort upon their sight and smell / no more banter / let's go pell-mell to meet in heaven or hand in hand in hell.

ALL: Smash! Splatter! Punch! Kick! Nut!

(MIKE *starts the words with a physical action appropriate to each word. The others take it up until it becomes a choreographic and vocal symbol of an advancing army. This action reveals a casualty – one of the lads from Mike's gang,* HARRY, *lies dying.*)

HARRY: Food for w-w-w- . . .

MIKE: Worms, Harry . . . worms . . .

RALPH: Quick, have it away / afore the law doth mark us for accessory!

(HARRY *dies. They race off, running on the spot, then turn upstage and run to their chairs, leaving Mike's mum and dad,* PEARL *and* SID, *with newspaper each side of the table.*)

Mike's mum and dad, SID *and* PEARL, *in their room.*

SID: It says here – pass another cuppa Pearl / that last night violent street gangs clashed / causing gevalt and misery / six taken in with wounds / one fatal / caused by they say / rough Gurkha knives and chains.

PEARL: It's not safe Sid to walk the streets at night / you'll want some more toast with your eggs?

SID: No, that's fine.

PEARL: A piece more cheese?

SID: Those lousy gits are getting bolder every day it makes you sick / the youth today / you got some Swiss?

53

PEARL: No, only Cheddar.

SID: That'll do / are all the fish cakes gone?

PEARL: You ate the last one yesterday.

SID: That's all you made!

PEARL: When I make more you leave them.

SID: So – they can't wait in the fridge and give a warm-up
    underneath the grill.

PEARL: Tomorrow I'll make some more.

SID: Then it's too late / my yen for fish cakes may be gone.

PEARL: That's why you leave them if I make a lot.

SID: 'Cause you don't tell there's some remaining / I always have
    to ask – you know I like them Pearl! A thousand curses on
    their guts those swine / the youth today / they don't know
    what to do but spraunce about.

PEARL: They're spoiled by overpay and telly.

SID: I should smile / filth that comes out streaming from the box
    and films!

LES: (*As chorus*) Shit, cunt-face, scabby bollocks.

SID: Ugh! You couldn't take like years ago your family out / to
    queue in one and nines and have a laugh / a sandwich in the
    bag to munch between the films.

PEARL: You'd always have a laugh.

SID: That's right / you're right / feel safe and cosy / where's little
    Mike?

PEARL: Bless him!

SID: He's tearing up and down the aisle / laugh! ice-cream from
    Wall's at twopence.

PEARL: Choc ices.

SID: Ice lollies.

PEARL: Vanilla cup.

SID: Chocolate whirl.

PEARL: Bag of peanuts.

SID: Never ate them / stuck in my dentures.

PEARL: I did.

SID: Yeah, you did / all the way through *Road to Bali*, munch,
    munch.

PEARL: *Road to Singapore*.

SID: *Road to Mandalay.*

PEARL: *Song of the Desert.*

SID: *Wizard of Oz.*

PEARL: *The Red Shoes.*

SID: Beautiful, beautiful, what a picture.

PEARL: *King Kong.*
> (CHORUS *mime end of* King Kong *sequence –* MIKE *on table as Kong and* CHORUS *as planes shooting at him.*)
> Get off the table, Mike, you'll upset your father.

SID: That was a shocker / a cuddle in the back.

PEARL: You never!

SID: Didn't I? Yes I did – and then we'd have a cuppa in Joe Lyons with a pastry / right / they'd make a great cuppa then.

PEARL: They were famous for it then.

SID: The pastries were delicious then.

PEARL: They made the best then.

SID: Rum baba / chocolate éclair.

PEARL: Custard tart.

SID: Lemon meringue.

PEARL: A gossip with our friends all content like don't see them any more.

SID: They don't visit.

PEARL: You don't ring them.

SID: They don't ring me / I should ring them!

PEARL: They should ring us.

SID: That's right – never ask about the kids / never say like years ago / come over Sid and have a cuppa, a game of solo and natter.

PEARL: You asked them once.

SID: I did / you're right / I won't keep begging them / I should beg them! / What have they done for me? I ask myself. Except to ask a favour.

PEARL: That's all.

SID: Hey Sid – lengthen a sleeve – Norman's grown out of them / take in a seat / you couldn't put a new lining in / could you?

PEARL: There's one in hospital who's still in coma fighting for his life.

SID: They get what they deserve / what they sow / they reap / they get as good as they give / I should worry for them? / An overstretched health service / and they get a bed at once / they should have let them bleed to death.

PEARL: He's still a son to some poor mother.

SID: Unwanted bastard of some brass no doubt / brought up by waiting by the pub.

LES: (*As chorus*) When we goin' home, Dad?

SID: Outside the door in all weathers / waiting for his dad and mum who's sinking down the pints inside / and now and then peek out to see the kids all right / buying them a bag of crisps to keep them happy / makes you sick / their little noses running / blue knees and shivering / while ma does . . .
(*Chorus sings 'Knees Up Mother Brown'.*)
. . . 'Knees Up Mother Brown' to some joanna that's the life they had / witness the clouts their mums have suffered at the hands of doltish drunken dad / and emulate the like as they turn into them in turn / coming home from school all starving with a bit of bread and dripping on the table and a note / do not disturb / while mum performs with 'uncle' up the stairs / breaking in and entry in their teens / and then a term or two of Borstal sets them up to be the citizens of our fair capital / when once we walked down Leicester's famous Square and had / the Corner House / a quartet playing / lunch at half a crown.

PEARL: Those were the days.

SID: The Salad Bowl.

PEARL: Mixed Grill.

SID: The Guinea and Piggy.

PEARL: All you could eat for a guinea / imagine.

SID: I kept going back for more / remember? he couldn't believe his eyes.

MIKE: (*As chorus*) You back again?

SID: Five times he saw me / fill it up I said / the plate was up to here / I wolfed it down though / went back again / all you could eat that's what it said / there's nothing they could do.

PEARL: They closed it down that's what they did.

SID: Not on account of me! 'Cause hard-faced layabouts would lay about at night / and put the wind up decent folks.

CHORUS: Hey Jimmy, gie's a drink!

SID: That's why they closed it mate / the West End's now a karzi. (*Chorus mimes vomiting.*)

SID: Now you dare not walk the streets at night / lest some unsavoury mugger / some huge shvartzer maybe / takes an eye to you.

CHORUS: What you lookin' at?

SID: Or drug-crazed hippie dying for a fix decides to stick a bayonet in your guts for half a dollar.

PEARL: I'm nervous going to bingo even and that's only down the road.

SID: Nobody phoned, eh?

PEARL: No, shall I ring Rosie / ask them round for tea on Sunday?

SID: We should ring them! When do they ring us?

PEARL: You're right Sid / you're quite right.

SID: Be independent / don't be proud to be a little independent.

PEARL: When you're right, you're right / maybe she rang and we were out.

SID: So did she try again? / You'll make fish cakes tomorrow.

PEARL: Yeah, I'll make a load / only who will eat them?

SID: I'll eat them / don't worry / I'll eat them!

Hospital. A bed. The face of HARRY, *dying, quite still. The table is the bed.*

LES: It was our fault that little Harry fell / his memory shall be honoured for all time / stabbed in the field by coward's hand.

RALPH: This will not go unanswered / he shall be avenged.

KEN: Eye for an eye / tooth for tooth.

LES: We had them on the run / they fled beneath our might / but one fell rat draws out a knife to leave his mark behind.

KEN: The canker of the nether world / they are a plague that we must crush / or else they'll grow / contaminate by touch.

RALPH: What's the answer / blood for blood?
    (*Music stops.*)

MIKE: You must strike at the top / cut off the head and then the

57

body's dead / confusion then will spread about / then we mop up / to get into the hornets' nest and kill the king / not battle in the streets / but plan concerted armed attack / he's hard you say / invincible to some / but he's only a human like us all / with feeling senses / if you kick him does he not hurt / if you stab him will he not bleed?

LES: To go into the lions' den is begging for it / they'll smell us at a mile / they'll see our homespun spotless faces / not scabby / lined with tracks like Clapham Junction / they'll sus us out before we're even near and wipe us off the streets.

MIKE: A little camouflage is what we need / divest yourselves of your smooth gear / and imitate the clobber of that mob / cheese-cutters and football boots / a choker round our neck in white / a black shirt here and there / and dirty up.

RON: That's great / I'll drink to that / let's make a ding-dong at Dave's pad to celebrate this plan / you're all invited / bring some booze the birds laid on / some slags he pulled from Dalston double-hot in keenness / and mad to make acquaintance of you Mike.

KEN: Yeah I double fancy that / right on mate / I'll change my knickers / let's get the booze.

MIKE: Do not forget what we have said tonight / don't let this booze-up blunt our dreaded purpose.

LES: Nay! / We will speak further on it / oh come on Mike / let's mix our grief with some small joy / to celebrate destruction of the beast / we'll make our plans tonight and fix the day!

MIKE: OK, at the Duke's Oak we meet / that's on the way.
(*Boys' pub talk:* 'Five pints, Bert.' 'Straight glasses, if you please.')

Mike's bird, SYLV, *in her room. Boys and family act as simultaneous background from their areas: pub at top;* PEARL *and* SID *in centre;* SYLV *at a bottom.*

SYLV: It was November / the last dead leaves of autumn / were falling off the perch / the day was cold as ice / flawless sky mind you / like it was washed in Daz / the pigeons picking at the hardened chunks of dogshit / it's silent, like a Sunday is round here / and I went down the road to get the *Sunday Mirror* / and some fags / the OAPs were snivelling in their scarves they wrap around their sunken sucked-in cheeks / as they bought cat food for their sole companions / their chat was shrill with 'Hallo Dot and how's your chest' and 'Innit parky, half a gallon of paraffin' / and back they went swaddled in veins and rheumatism to their grim / stove on the landing / room / cold water and a pic of dad / when he was fighting for his king for three and six a week / a postcard on the mantelpiece from daughter seen just once a year / at Xmas maybe / or a death / it's funny that I sit in now and wait for him to ring / he said he would today.

MIKE: Go on, Les. Put something on the jukebox.

LES: What d'ya want – Rosemary Clooney?

PEARL: Must we watch telly all the time? Let's play cards.

SYLV: Mike usually decides to come over / that's so nice / we sit in watching some old flic on telly / or playing Perry Como or some Brahms particularly he likes the Fifth by Beethoven / it gets him all worked up he says though / I like dancing really to some Latin / we jump around a bit and shake a leg / we'll have a fag or two / or smoke a joint / maybe a benny just before our lunch / I'll warm a frozen curry from the store / maybe Fray Bentos / though Chinese from the takeaway is nice / some chop suey and some chips / that's good, I fancy that and he don't half love it as well / I'll get that in a minute and what else / I think that's all . . . oh come on Mike and bloody phone you bloomin' bore.

MIKE: Not too much, Ken.

LES: Five more pints, Bert.

SID: Oh my ulcer! Pulverize a couple of pills, Pearl!

SYLV: Suppose I get it all and he don't come / I'll keep it for tomorrow / I'll do that he ain't half nice – really he is / he has his funny ways / I mean who don't / and sometimes I could strangle him / but when he looks at me with those hurt eyes / I just want then to mother him / he's really handsome like a movie star / but rugged like not poofy but a cross between Paul Newman and Brando / with little hints of Redford and a touch of Cary Grant or maybe Boris Karloff / he don't half make me laugh sometimes / we'd laugh so much they'd knock back on our walls / those from next door – that woman who is always sick and lives with her mad son who never works / oh come on Mike.

MIKE: So go on, ask me: do I care?

BOYS: Do you care?

PEARL: Dorothy said she might pop in tonight.

SID: I'm out!

SYLV: I can't remember did I take the pill today or not / oh piss I lost my little card / oh never mind / but then suppose he wants to then what do I do / oh never mind one day won't hurt or will it / no I shouldn't think it would / or would it / rules are rules and if you break them then you take the risk – men! Much they care – but then they're not supposed to – really / they never do.

STEVE: Seein' Sylv tonight?

MIKE: Nah. Givin' her the elbow.

LES: How about Ange?

PEARL: Turn it off, for Christ's sake.

SID: It's the weather forecast.

SYLV: I can't go through all that again / no God forbid / I just can't go back to that vile place / and let them in to murder part of me again / like opening your doors to killers in white coats and saying / it's in there – you will be quick / it won't hurt it – will it? / No! No! Not again / oh come on Mike I'm getting bored hanging around – it's Sunday – come on ring you sod.

RALPH: So I said, pal, do I look like a tin of dog food?

SID: Go to bed.

(SYLV *takes fag out – looks in mirror. Lifts her skirt – suspender belt, garters.*)

SYLV: Couldn't resist it really – he likes that – it's cheeky / I feel funny in the street / funny and nice at once / to know what's underneath / and no one else suspects / how could they / I'll give him a surprise / that's if he wants surprising that is / don't know lately if it's getting / well . . . / better or worse / can never tell with him / or maybe he's getting something

else to play with / bastard bet he has / oh if he dares! Maybe
that's it / it's wearing out / it's not the armed assault like once
it was / then he'd come at me like I was the last bird in the
world / he said he loved me then / after the op he turned all
funny for a while / chop suey or a curry – maybe a plate o
spags / oh ring you git I can't stay in all day and wait and
wait.

LES: Here's to a smooth and slick funeral!

PEARL: It's just a blank screen, Sid!

SYLV: I fancy going up West / I'll treat him to a film and we'll sit
in a nice wine bar / I'd like to meet some people / for a
change / just watch them even / sick of staying in / oh come
on, ring me, please ring! Please ring – please ring.

RALPH: Do you all know the way to Dave's? First right, first left.

PEARL: I'm going to bed.

The gang at a table – harsh white light.

MIKE: A score of broken bones and busted shnozzles was the
price we paid by being unprepared.

RALPH: By being unprepared we was caught out with knickers
well and truly down.

STEVE: They came back for revenge last night / for the almighty
pasting that they took as if poor Harry's precious life was not
enough to slake the creature's thirst.

LES: The brute and monstrous thing rose from its lair into the
thick sulphurous night / while we were snoring gorged
appetites like swinish pigs / well bloated and obscene from
'evening in' with favoured bints / their perfumed limbs
enwrapped us like some marble seraphims / the sweetttnness
of their breath, so honeydewed mellifluous with tinkling
flute-like voices / beguiled us with soft porn suggestions / in
the dales and valleys of our ears / and we unpeeled them like
it was a ripened plum or mango – satsuma or sweet pear. But
they were poisoned fruit / within they carried venom /
between their loins a praying mantis / sucking us to our death
in lust-filled swoons / for they had plans / the birds we pulled
last night were fronted to attack / were set up to assuage us in

our guard by rendering unarmed our finest men / attacking
us where we are vulnerable / our sensual centres / famed to all
the world / those cornucopias of passion / our Achilles' heel /
our Samson's hair / where flock the sirens of the Western
world / to feed and drink in our rich pastures / welcoming
them all / turning none from our door / those starved within
the barren regions / of Dalston, Enfield and Wood Green /
who flocked to Stamford Hill.

MIKE: Oh horro! Horror! Horror!

RALPH: We planned too late our deed / we should have struck
when he was bloated in his bed as he found us / instead of
deeds / we fell to carousing as if to celebrate the victory
before it's won.

MIKE: Oh you my sinews bear me stiffly up!

RALPH: We were a cinch / lucky for you that you were out / the
stroke of fate that did decide by tossing coins / you were the
chosen one to buy the shish kebab from takeaway / or else
you may have suffered that like fate / that marched so
painfully upon our undefended loins.

MIKE: My fate cries out and makes each petty artery in this body
as hardy as the hardest villain's nerve / I'll tear him all to
pieces!

ALL: You shall not go.

MIKE: Unhand me / by heaven I'll make a corpse of him that lets
me / I say away! I warned you / what did I say! You were
seduced by snatch / your watchman fast asleep / his potion
drugged no doubt / allowed yourselves to be disarmed and
floating in the ether of vile lust / so's not to hear the hobnail
boots they always wear with toes steelcapped in dread / you
mugs / what are you / with friends like you I don't need
enemies / you were outshrewded by the Hoxton fiends /
who's celebrating now, no doubt in City Arms / carousing
with his chinas of / how easy it was after all / and laughing
with loud chortles / while the blast of shame sits on our
brows like the ill mark of Cain / now who comes here?
(*A* MESSENGER *approaches.*)

MESSENGER: I come unarmed from Hoxton's mighty King / to

give a message to him that calls himself / the Prince of
Darkness / the King of Stamford Hill or just plain Shtip-it-in
Mike.

MIKE: I'm known by many names but those will do / say what
your business is and blow / you emissary from the
underworld where sunshine never comes and days are
choked in hell's polluted smoke / say what brings you here to
gloat upon your master's cowardice and treachery.

MESSENGER: Cut out the patter man and cock an ear to what my
honoured master hath to spout.

LES: You dare to speak like that you pint of gnat's piss.

MIKE: Let him go.

MESSENGER: And wisely said / that you may learn a thing or
three / I see you are the guvnor / so here's the spiel / to cut all
these wars which doth confuse the citizens of our strife-warm
manor / to halt the battles in the Royal Tottenham which
hath us banned from dancing with our chicks / and making
parley with our mates / to cease the clash of skull and iron in
our streets which doth excite old johnny law to exercise his
tool on us / and bring the black marias out like wailing
banshees / round our council flats / in other words a one to
one / just you and he – step round the back – by some remote
deserted track / the Hackney marshes / or designate a place
that you prefer / I'll pass the message on.

MIKE: The marshes suits me well / tell him I'll come.

MESSENGER: Upon the stroke of twelve / one week from now.

MIKE: I shall be there.

(MESSENGER *exits*.)

LES: I do not doubt some foul play.

MIKE: A one to one / it's what I've always dreamed of.

KEN: What if he should lure you into some forbidden trap and
there . . . phut!

MIKE: What should I fear / when I now sense a giant strolling in
my veins / now I could slay whole armies all alone / a one to
one / I wish there were a hundred just like he / a week from
now / till then sit still my soul / for Hackney marshes will
become the bloody sea.

(*They trot off in quasi-military fashion. Exeunt. Fanfare.*)

SID *and* PEARL *in their room. They speak but not to each other.*

SID: Soho's not what it's cut out to be.

PEARL: I get bored watching telly every night.

SID: There was a time when it was fun to walk the streets in
summer / birds out on the game / all legs / then to stand
about / flaunt themselves for all to see / you knew what you
were getting / not that I got / but for a laugh you'd ask how
much / and go up to the next / it passed the time.

PEARL: Sometimes I'd like to pack my bags and leave him to it /
just run out and go / I don't care where / just up and off / and
never see his face again / it's too late now / I should have done
it long ago.

SID: Where did it go wrong I ask myself / she never had to do a
stroke of work / I brought home all my wages every week /
not all mind you but they never went short.

PEARL: He's not taken me out in years / not once in years like /
come on Pearl let's drive to Brighton for the day . . .
(*Tableau as* BOYS *and* SYLV *join in and re-create the scene.*) . . .
it's sunny out / we'll pack a lunch and take the kids I used to
like it years ago / the pier and stroll along the prom / sit on
the beach and watch Michael throw pebbles in the sea / and
then a game of housey housey it's called bingo now / we won
a silver-plated teapot . . . (*Scene disappears.*) . . . where has it
gone I wonder?

SID: The others all made profits from the war / I was an honest
joe / I could have made a fortune / with a little simple graft /
black market was the rage.

PEARL: But for the kids / I'd have slipped out long ago / but when
you're tied it's difficult / how could I leave them / or support
them in a furnished room / it's just for them I live – it's for
the twinkle in my baby's eye that I can soldier on / not that
he's an angel but he's all I got / and she's as good as gold.

SID: They're ingrates that's the truth / give us a quid or two dad /
or a tenner / or a pony maybe / pay you back? No never /
sponge on my old bones till I drop dead / I'd like for once to

see him looking smart / a decent hair cut / a well-cut suit
instead of that costume he wears / the layabout.

PEARL: I look at him and think what have I got but habit and some
sleeping pills / to send us to oblivion at night or ease the pain of
our arthritic bones / to soften his loud snores and give an hour
or two of sweet forgetfulness / one day I'll take the lot.

SID: Harry's boy did well / matriculated and all that / then
college / then degree in this and that / and a clever lad /
stopped in most every night to fill his cop with knowledge /
he's no shmuck / and the skill to stand up in a court and be a
man / defending companies in the quagmire of business
laws / what a man is Harry's boy / his mum and dad he
bought a home in Chingford with a garden and drives a Ford
estate / what did my son achieve for us – gevalt and anguish
fear for every knocking on the door / in case some johnny law
should say we're looking for . . .

PEARL: Some wives have husbands who's a joy / so proud they
entertain / and lay a table for their friends on Sunday
night . . .
(*Party tableau*. 'Hello, lovely to see you', *etc*.)
. . . a drink of port / and tell some jokes / maybe a game of
pontoon / silver laid / and lumps of children everywhere /
daughters and sons / grandchildren too / to fuss over / their
grannies take them out / their fathers proud and braying the
achievements in the world of their most honoured kids / they
don't invite us any more . . .

LES: 'Bye, Aunty Pearl.

SYLV: Lovely meringues, Pearl.

MIKE: Ring you.

PEARL: . . . and I can't go alone / he says he's too tired to go out /
and what have they done for him he says / you've only got to
entertain them back / so we sit in and watch the telly.

SID: I showed him how to earn an honest buck / I only told him /
get out now and graft / did I do something wrong / to turn
him to a villain / lousy sponger / low-life that he is / who
comes home when he does with busted teeth and broken
bones and God knows where he's been or what he's done / if

he stayed in and copped a book or two or got a decent job
when he was young instead of dancing out all night with
stinking whores no doubt / the filth he mixes with is rife in
bad contagion / if he had worked he's got some brain / he
could have been a manager at least of Cecil Gee's / or maybe
an accountant / Tucker that's a job! For that you need a
noddle in your bonce / faa! A pervert for a son / to tell the
truth no blood of mine but hers.

PEARL: He set him no example if he's bad.

SID: From her and all her spoiling he's no good.

PEARL: When did he get a father's love / I ask myself.

SID: She always favoured him / right from the moment he was
born.

PEARL: He never took an interest in him the way a father should /
to show him what it is that he should know.

SID: What time does *Hawaii Five-O* come on?

PEARL: Eight o'clock.

SID: Turn it on, will you love?

GROUP: I fancy going down the Royal / I double fancy that / the
Mecca is my temple of fate / who shall I pull / who shall I
meet, will she be wrapped up like a Xmas treat / the fireball
is turning, the music starts / your eyes survey the crumpet /
and you say, do you wanna dance, do you wanna dance?

BOYS: Do ya wanna dance?

(MIKE *takes* SYLV *on to the floor, just the two of them. The* BOYS
are upstage, acting as a chorus line with invisible partners.)

MIKE: Do you wanna dance / we slid on to the floor like two seals
in a pool / wearing an ashen look about her face / smelling
like a perfume counter at Boots / she had that look about
her / like I couldn't care if you dropped dead look / her eyes
scanning other talent / searching out the form / of course we
do not get too close / just enough to give a hint of things to
come / a lasso of lust waves encircles her.

SYLV: He . . . he looks like any other / with easy grin / street-
corner patter / so we dance a bit and then he asks me.

MIKE: Do you fancy a drink?

SYLV: With him / as if he bought me / for a dance / whereas I stand
or sit with or without mates / watching lines of faceless
trousers stomping up and down.

MIKE: She looks nice.

SYLV: He looks O K / nice eyes / love crumbled grey / and smoking
already for me / he says he don't half fancy taking me home /
back to my gaff / an arm squeezed.

MIKE: Fancy her / not much I don't half.

SYLV: Yeah another gin and it / lipstick smudged / I'll do my hair /
excuse me.

ALL: Thanks luv / that was nice / enjoyed that / fancy a drink /
where d'ya live? – oh!

MIKE: I got to the karzi / full of geezers doing their barnets and who
has who.

STEVE: I'll take the ugly one.

LES: Yeah all right!

KEN: What a cracker.

RALPH: I didn't get nothin'!

MIKE: And all that / I take the future of England in my hand and
ponder her body which seems to me as if a shoal of silvery fish
were gathered in a net / and wiggling and slithery and her
silken skin encasing her incredible form.

LES: Mind the strides, pal.

MIKE: Whilst I read what Kilroy has been up to / so after much chat
and I don't know / the night was wearing thin and I became
afeared that unless she yielded to my heart-felt quest / to take
her home that is / these chicks / these panoplies of exquisite
and sensual delights / would be booked up by other snatch-
bandits staking out their prey for the night and if at twelve
o'clock I walk home on my tod sloan I would be well and truly
choked.

SYLV: Not tonight, let it not be tonight.

MIKE: All right just to the door / unless . . .

SYLV: No, I said not tonight.

MIKE: Why wait / what makes it better if you wait / it's cold out
here / let's go inside / her make-up's cracked beneath the
light / our breath steams and snorts.

SYLV: He should wait / else I'm just another receptacle to stomp
out his butt / he pushes himself against me like I was for him a
sanctuary that he was struggling to get into.

MIKE: Like I was pursued by wolves / and she took my breath away.

SYLV: And he asked me out next day / and from then on all I wanted
was to be a sacrifice / like an offering / I can't help it / how
often can you feel that / and that's how I felt / and he felt good
to me all the time / and often / not like the others but someone
wanting someone like me / and now why won't the bastard
ring?

The lads jump in attacking stance.

MIKE: Like stepping round the back was what was expected of
you / like a clobbering now and then / was mixed up with
pulling birds round there for stand-up charvers / like that very
spot where now you gaily spray your spunk / was where two
nights ago you splattered blood / 'gainst that very wall / you
pulled in passageways / in doorways / in any nook and cranny
so you'd only exercise your passion in the dark and private /
with a bird / or bloke for violence or love / or be in love with
violence / so when two tearaways decide to bundle / to inflict
some GBH upon each other's form / they might be making
love / and seeking out the soft parts to inflict upon them some
unsightly woe / and finish off the night in blissful satisfaction /
of adrenalin well pumped and flushy bleeding faces / all lit up
with joy / and many hand thumps on the back.

STEVE: You did all right, mate.

LES: Yes? / you din half give him one / boot in like –

RALPH: Kicked the shit out of –

KEN: I like the bit when –

STEVE: Well and truly.

LES: Handsome / ta da!

STEVE: See ya!

LES: Look after –

KEN: See you, plater.

RALPH: All the brest.

KEN: So he decided that it had to be and so prepared himself for the onslaught / toe to toe and nose to nose / the weapons chosen / and us chinas to be there in case the others thrust their grubby maulers in.

Gym. MIKE *training with weights / during this last speech / pushing weights in conjunction with music / muscles bulging / veins swelling / sweat pouring off in shower / the mates continuing their foreboding text.*

RALPH: I've seen the brutish thing he has to slay fancy his chances / I don't know / I hate to tell my mucker / my best mate / that I might carry in my heart / a little doubt / so I'll keep shtoom / and render him my total confidence in this night's caper.

LES: The other bloke annihilated last week / was in a coma for some days / between the sheets he bled / and put tubes in both his ears / to see if he was leaking red from broken tissues / or the brain / that's what they do / and shoved up little things into his nose in case he haemorrhaged and formed a clot and shaved his head and searched his skull in case his mind was cracked / or broken / but he recovered to tell the tale.

STEVE: And was it worth it after all / I'd be rather all tucked up and wrapped around a softer creature / dragging kisses up from the deep / than face a bunch of fives well clenched / I do not fancy kissing that at all.

MIKE: But who can undo what has been done / or wipe the writing off from on the wall / what has to be will be.

Walking home after the gym, bag over shoulder. Music. Each one follows the other and takes over the walk.

RALPH: Walking home alone beneath the stars / up Amhurst Road / to Manor House / and down to Finsbury Park / where little ducks sit quietly at night / like toys in a lake of glass / to lonely back streets after / nights of rock and roll at the Rainbow / or James Bond giving her one at the Essoldo / maybe a binge at some vomity local / going home in pairs / to make it in the back of steamed-up Minis / I could not help but wonder on this night of all the talent getting well and

truly laid / and all the grinding going on / and how many and
how much / and all the wails and screaming going on right at
this moment / could almost in the silent aching streets / hear
across the city all the sighs / rising and falling like sirens /
thousands, maybe tens of thousands creating a vast and
lubricious symphony / a concerto / and in the secret places /
alleyways and back rooms at parties / some in crispy beds /
and some round backs of lorries or in graveyards / some
getting their oats before their time / by dint of threat / in
lonely fields / dragged there by snatch-crazed fiends.

LES: Digging in and hacking away like crazy robbers / smash and
grab of flesh / and tides rising and falling together / while the
mad moon / a giant's eye spying it all out / the murdered and
the robbed / and geezers out for bondage in Earls Court / and
in the night the steam is rising / from the heaps of bodies
twisted in shapes like vampires feasting on their prey / and
the cars passing / occupants all warm and cosy / he's driving /
Zappa in stereo / hand on knee / maybe one will stop for me /
and some delicious and horrendous piece / swathed in filth-
packed flesh will utter / can I give you a lift young man /
drooling sibilantly from scarlet lush-filled lips / opens the
door / smelling like honeysuckle in the dark the hint of
things to come / the promise of Elysium / and we'll shoot off
into the night searching for treasure.

KEN: But nothing / only the jeers of dawn carousers heading for
their unmade beds in Walthamstow and Leyton / reeking
stale beer and fish and chips / Fray Bentos pies from all-night
stands in Spitalfields / then home belching their unholy gut
rot into their scummy slags that hang around hair lacquered
like Brillo pads / and waking in the light of day / one white
arm / with digital / cheap one upon his wrist comes snaking
out the pit where scrubber lies a-snoring.

STEVE: And searching in his trousers for a pack of fags / starts the
day in cough-wake / dragging ropes of phlegm / from vaults
well stocked within / blue smoke rising / while the sunshine
peeks reluctantly in / exposing a big juicy yellow pimple on
her back / comes then spewing through the radio some idiot /

so the day starts in a bath of rancid bacon and eggs.

MIKE: I'll get into my little bed / thus strengthened by steel for the battle ahead / I'll drink a pint / say my prayers / and wait for mum to wake me in the morning / French toast and tea / I double fancy that.

ACT TWO

Song of the Hoxton Mob. They march around the stage with East End macho-animalistic precision, jutting heads and threatening stares, to a drum beat.

CURLY:
> I'm known as the avenger / when
> they see me they do quell / for
> they see before their runny
> eyes a short pathway to ultra-
> violence / with a swift descent to hell.
>
> They scare before they get here /
> they tremble at my name / to look
> upon my face is quite enough to
> send them packing off before
> they've time to clench their
> sweaty fists to deal out pain.
>
> I'm known as the avenger / and they
> seek to claim my crown / but the
> hardest villains are the ones that
> soonest / come tumbling down.
>
> So come on boy / I'm waiting
> I hear you're on your way /
> I'm hungry for the blood of
> victims / I need another jerk
> like you / a mama's boy to slay.

MIKE *jumps into a pool of light and becomes a Cockney Lenny Bruce for five minutes.*

MIKE: Every day in the morning – while the sun rose like a biscuit
> behind the glue factory / quivering in the smoke / I'd get up

at seven to go to work mum packs some sandwiches / which
would get soggy by the time it was opened / I would crush
myself in the tube and others behind me would crush and
we'd all get crushed together / which was all right if you
happened to have your leg wedged between the thighs of
some radiant fair-skinned blushing and divine darling but
not if some stinking gentleman from an exotic country of the
East was breathing the shit he calls food all over your face /
and as the doors slid open this composite mass of sludgy flesh
would wobble like a wall of jelly / and some schemer would
put a foot in the door and attempt to weld himself into the
compost heap quivering together / on the Piccadilly Line
poo! who farted? was it you? I'd read the latest filth scrawled
up when the doors open no one would move to let anyone in /
we were staunch allies in our square foot of space / the doors
shut and the pack got squirmicr / I was thinking about that
bundle all the while and making horrible little flickers in my
mind about the outcome / eyes staring into their daily tits
that they'll never feel only ogle / hands would wander about
in the pit of hell / old ladies gasping their last breath / glaring
at some young sod in a seat / and umbrella stuck up your ass /
fags stubbed out in your face / and the ads advised you on the
merits of speedwriting / revealing some grotty slag smiling
deliriously like an insane gorilla / while chewing on an
improvised cock drawn by a future Picasso / and I stare all
the time at the ads like it was a meditation / while performing
frottage against a piece of taffeta / lovely / working as typist
in Oxford Street / oh no, don't get out yet / I'm not there yet /
you may not be dear but I am! / oh sod it / Oxford Circus /
and the train heaves us like a bad case of diarrhoea / then I'm
channelled up the elevator still holding my dangle / and
briefcase with the squashed-up sandwiches / churned up like
the debris of human rejects / bits of machinery on the
conveyer belt going back for repairing / or destroying / and I
hoped I'd see that bird again / she was lovely with great
gooey eyes / maybe I'll wait for her tomorrow / wend my way
to my office in Bond Street where I was a managing director

of a firm of wholesale jewellers / flogging pearls out of a
suitcase in Oxford Street for Xmas (genuine three-strung
diamanté pearls / a quid / with beautiful engine-turned,
bevelled edges) / come on don't just stand there / gentleman
over there / lady over there / watch out there's a johnny / nip
into Woolie's or the ABC for a quick cup of bird vomit /
travelling salesmen swilling down some unidentified goo /
grins stitched to their unfortunate faces / collapsed spine /
frayed cuffs and souls / and breath to fell a dragon / I saw a
geezer shove his fork into a pie at one of these filling stations /
of garbage manufacturers / but it was empty except for a
mouse that was curled up inside with a happy look on his
face / sleeping / and he didn't want to disturb the mouse like
he thought it could have been a pet / since a lot of these chain
cafés have a lot of mice around / so he took it back / this
mouse has eaten my pie miss / he said / this waitress who was
slithering around in the dead grease / with bunches of
varicose like gnarled roots on her pins / says: what and it's
still alive! / I'm glad something likes our pies / here never
mind the humour I want another pie / he was sweating now
since he used this day's voucher up / she says I'll send it back
to the makers and if they find it faulty they'll refund your
money / but this didn't solve the problem / and he screamed
that they didn't need to send it back / the evidence is there in
the mouse / so after all the rhubarb and shouting / he's
kicking up a big pen and ink / the manager comes sludging
over / a fag hanging out of his head / and one off his ear / and
one up his ass no doubt / so this greasy manager comes
wiping his fingers on his apron / since he'd been making ham
sandwiches / had distinguished himself in service by cutting
the thinnest ham in the world / and was straightaway
employed by Forte's / so here he was and said if you make a
fuss like this in a good British café / three million men fought
the Second World War on food like this / so the salesman
bowing to his superior size says all right / and the manager
seeing that the salesman had calmed down said / was there
something he could do for him / and the salesman brightened

up a bit says / perhaps you could warm the mouse up please /
certainly sir, right away sir, came the immediate response /
but the mouse sussing something is up with all the
movement going on cocks an ear and runs down the
waitress's leg / she screamed / farted loudly enough to shake
the windows and slides over on the greasy floor / keeling over
a table on the way down / whose aged occupants were
shocked into a sudden coma / well after that I didn't fancy
going back to that café any more / it's all true / don't look at
me like that / I'm worried about that fight / anyway I gave up
flogging bent gear in Oxford Street after that / they say
there's a big future in flogging magistrates with bags over
their heads / they pay well.

(*They all mime a tube in rush hour, the words of the* CHORUS
syncopating with the train:)

ALL: Breakfast, shit, work, lunch, bed.

*Back on the tube or walking the streets – slow motion – best on the tube
– only a few strap-hangers or passers-by become* MIKE's *friends.*

LES: Hallo Mike / I wish you luck for tomorrow.

MIKE: Thanks.

RALPH: How do you think you'll do?

MIKE: Very well thank you / how's your mother?

RALPH: She's OK.

MIKE: Still washing your knickers?

RALPH: No fear / I send them to be read by a fortune-teller.

LES: Are you scared?

MIKE: Not a jot / not a jot.

LES: I bet you are.

MIKE: How much / wanna see my pants?

SYLV: Don't go Mike / they're goading you on.

MIKE: What are you doing on the Piccadilly Line?

SYLV: Giving head to accountants in the rush hour.

MIKE: That's not very nice / is it?

SYLV: I waited in all day for you Sunday.

MIKE: I had things on my mind.

SYLV: That's what they all say.

MIKE: Who's they?

SYLV: I wish I knew.

STEVE: Going down the Royal tonight?

MIKE: I can't / gotta preserve my strength.

STEVE: Pity, we had something really dishy lined up for you.

MIKE: Keep it warm for me under the grill / I'll be back.

STEVE: You hope.

MIKE: What do you mean?

STEVE: Oh words words words.

MIKE: They're trying to undermine my fierce endeavour.

KEN: Hello Mike / coming for a ride up West?

MIKE: Not tonight Ken / not tonight old son.

KEN: Who's going with you Mike?

MIKE: I'll go alone unless you want to hold my coat.

KEN: Do me a favour / I wouldn't go down there for all the salmon in Wentworth Street.

(*All except* MIKE *leave the train.* PEARL *and* SID *get on.*)

SID: You could have been an accountant or a manager of a string of menswear shops.

MIKE: I'd rather be bounded in a nutshell and count myself king of infinite space.

PEARL: Michael, my son, my joy and pride / jewel of my loins / apple of my eye / the be-all and end-all / the sun in the morning and the stars at night / where are you going my son?

MIKE: For a fight to the death / a battle of honour / destruction of a monster / to kill the plague / to slay the dragon / to defend the weak / to prove my worth / to destroy the mighty / to avenge the dead / to annihilate the oppressor / to be a mensh / to have a punch-up.

PEARL: Well wrap up warm / it's bitter out.

SID: Come on, Mum.

(*They leave the train.*)

MIKE: Stars hide your fires / let night not see my dark and deep desires / maybe I'll go dancing after all to keep my mind off it.

The CHORUS *is seated as in a dance hall.* MIKE *takes* SYLV *into the centre of the floor. Gradually the others dance around them, holding invisible partners.*

MIKE: Do you wanna dance / I took her on the floor / the crystal ball smashed the light into a million pieces / a shattered lake at sunrise / the music welled up / and the lead guitarist / plugged into ten thousand watts zonging in our ears / callused thumb whipping chords / down the floor we skate / I push her thigh with mine / and backwards she goes to the gentle signal / no horse moved better / and I move my left leg which for a second leaves me hanging on her thigh / then she moves hers / swish / then she's hanging on mine / like I am striding through the sea / our thighs clashing and slicing past each other like huge cathedral bells / whispering past flesh-encased nylon / feeling / all the time knees / pelvis / stomach / hands / fingertips / grip smell / moving interlocking fingers / ice floes melting / skin silk weft and warp / blood-red lips gleaming / pouting / stretching over her hard sharp and wicked-looking Hampsteads / words dripping out her red mouth gush like honey / I lap it up / odours rising from the planet of the flesh / gardens after light showers / hawthorn and wild mimosa / Woolie's best / crushed fag ends / lipstick / powder / gin and tonic / all swarming together on one heavenly nerve-numbing swill / meanwhile huge mountains of aching fleshy worlds are drifting past each other holding their moons / colliding and drifting apart again / the light stings / the journey is over / the guitarist splattered in acne as the rude knife of light stabs him crushes his final shattering chord / the ball of fire stops / and I say thank you very much.

SYLV: OK.

MIKE: Speak again, bright angel.

SYLV: I fink I'll have a gin and tonic.

LES: You're avoiding your destiny by diversions.

MIKE: Tomorrow and tomorrow . . .

SYLV: I waited for you all day Sunday.

MIKE: I had something on my mind.

SYLV: Come on home / I'll cook you a plate of spags.

MIKE: I'd rather eat the air promise-crammed.

SYLV: You must be starving.

MIKE: I'm preparing myself for the battle on Sat.

SYLV: Will you come over after?

MIKE: Yes long after / if I am here.

SYLV: Are you scared?

MIKE: Not a jot.

SYLV: Why are you so mean / you told me you loved me once.

MIKE: You were the more deceived.

SYLV: Heaven help him.

LES: Oh blessed Mike / why art thou not in constant training for the event?

MIKE: How do you know what I do all day / who watches my mental exercise / detects the secret plans I make / an armoury of weapons / stored in the forceful regions of my brain / I'll hypnotize the beast / and psych him out / drinks all round.

LES: Here's to the end of the Hoxton King.

RALPH: Destruction of the stinking dragon.

STEVE: The ogre falls.

KEN: Hideous and most sweet revenge.

LES: No more trembling in the strasser.

RALPH: Pull the birds we like.

STEVE: Safe conduct to the supermarkets.

KEN: Unimpeded entry to the Essoldo.

LES: Sleep tight at nights.

RALPH: Noisy mouthpieces / no frighteners.

STEVE: No knifing from bumper cars at Battersea.

KEN: Our motorbikes safe from slashing tyres.

LES: No more dreaded smells.

RALPH: No more terrified cats.

STEVE: Shaking OAPs.

MIKE: The Hackney marshes.

ALL: The Hackney marshes.

PEARL: You could have been had you tried / a manager / a solicitor / or even a representative of a firm of ladies' underwear manufacturers / your uncle would help you / I'm sure you would have liked getting into ladies' underwear /

look at your cousin Willy.

STEVE: Wife – three kids – responsibilities.

KEN: House in Colindale.

SID: Detached.

LES: Mark 2 Cortina – £15,000 a year.

(*They follow* MIKE *as he runs away from the train of responsibility that pursues him, and they circle stage and sit.* MIKE *whips round and makes a speech to the audience.*)

MIKE: Why should I yoke myself to nine to five / stand shoulder to shoulder with the dreary gang who sway together in the tube / or get acquainted with parking meters / be a good citizen of this vile state / so I can buy an ultra-smart hi-fi and squander fortunes on pop singles / what do you do at night between the sheets but dream of mortgages and oh dear the telly's on the blink / we're going to Majorca again this year / you who've never raped a virgin day / with adrenalin assault upon your senses / but aggravate your spine to warp / while grovelling for a buck / or two / smiling at your boss / and spend heart-wrenched hours at the boutique deciding what to wear / ragged up like Chelsea pooftahs / or chase some poor mutt on Sundays / mad keen to commit some GBH upon it / and birds like screaming hyenas with teeth and scarves flying / make your usual boring death-filled chat in smelly country pubs / with assholes like yourself / no that's not for me / I'd rather be toad and live in the corner of a dungeon for other's uses.

The HOXTON GANG *with their leader,* CURLY. *They appear to lean against a lamp post, each facing out, like four gargoyles, a hard light from overhead.*

CURLY: Night and silence / that's what it's all about.

BURT: You're right Curly / oh son of night – the atmosphere is double-strong / star-filled / the perfect evening for a fight.

PAT: It's what you need / a cobbled street / just wet a bit / to give a little image of a broken moon / a yellow lamplight / flickering a bit / still lit in gas.

REG: The echo of our studs on lonely streets / the smoke of

cigarettes / thickening in a blast of light / like fiery dragons /
in our lair we hover / smelling blood / our leathern wings
glistening in the dewy air.

CURLY: The odd moth hanging about / and eyeing up the scene /
banging his fretful wings / oh let me in it says / to the hungry
flame.

BURT: Then out he goes / like a light double-choked / to be so
scorched up.

PAT: Right burnt up he was about it.

ALL: Laughter – cackle – silence.

CURLY: In just such a manner doth our fretful moth of Stamford
Hill / bang against the light that we give out / he wants to be
let in / and then . . .

PAT: Phhht!

CURLY: We wait / we've time / I don't think he will be late / I
sense him now weighing up the scales of chance / thinking
thick regrets / and oh what a mug am I, swallow it, he thinks,
turn yellow / at least you'll keep your face / the one the birds
do like to chase / you'll lose the other / the one you'll never
again show to mates.

PAT: He's as chicken as a chicken coming to a fox / his pants hot
lined in shit / I hear / that fear has wrenched from out his
guts.

BURT: He does it to be king of his bankrupt domain / to cancel
out the bum he is at home / so he can spout out to the world
that he's got clout / and make the teenyboppers moist their
flowers / and holler, oh Michael / so he can stand up West
and join the firm of grievous / rape / robbery and death /
solicitors to the realm.

PAT: He desperately wants his diploma / and that is you / to
launch him on the path of hate / that's lined in gelt and not a
caper down the Ly / a bundle for a laugh / but turn pro /
that's his game.

CURLY: I'll not disappoint him / I am guaranteed against default /
reckless in my desire to give value / fear no marks upon my
well-worn face / have nought to save / but welcome all / I'll
make love to him / my caresses will start their long journey in

hell / he'll not see it coming / only feel / I'll embrace him like
a hungry bear / my hands will find his body's treats / and
practise on his bones / we'll dance and then I'll look into his
eyes / wet with tears of thankfulness / as I do renovate the
house he lives in / he'll whisper like a gasping lover / to the
background of splintering sounds / as he hears the music of
his body's walls snap and crack / his heart will beat a terrible
drum / and want to burst to spread some numbing death
relieving darkness / so come on scum.

The café of Mike's mates.

LES: Two teas, Joe.

JOE: Sugar?

LES: One, ta.

RALPH: Got any sandwiches?

JOE: Sold out.

RALPH: Do you suppose it's possible to organize one?

JOE: Not now.

RALPH: Why not?

JOE: Because it's late.

RALPH: Ah, go on, don't be a fat pig.

JOE: Closing.

LES: Sod you, you slimy middle-aged fart.

RALPH: I hope you starve / the time will come when nobody
comes in this dung heap and your family is condemned to
catch rats to eat / while your children crawl in lice and your
wife's hair falls out / may your daughters be gang-raped by
blacks / and your house burnt down with your kids
screaming / while you sit here counting your gelt you
scheming piece of dogshit.
(*Record on juke-box: 'You are the sunshine of my life'.*)

JOE: All right I'll make you a sandwich / what do you want?

RALPH: Roast beef and coleslaw in toasted brown.

JOE: Just watch it / next time you'll go too far and say something
you'll regret, OK?

STEVE: Half-hour to go / Mike cut his hair and greased it / he can't
grip that / so as to introduce his knee upon Mike's head.

KEN: That's shrewd.

STEVE: We should have been there / we should.

RALPH: Then why weren't we / case the others jump him if he's out in front?

STEVE: Dunno.

RALPH: You're his mate aren't you?

STEVE: Well, so are you.

RALPH: Yeah.

STEVE: He's mad to go / what does it prove / to swallow it's no shame / we know Mike's tough / ignore those bums / that's what I say.

KEN: He'll swallow nothing / so he'll taste nothing bitter in his mouth like us / he goes because he has to / and for us / you know that's true / he goes for you!

SID *comes downstage, alone.*

SID: Once in Soho, a while ago, round the back streets / walking one night to catch the tube I wandered round the alleyways / a saunter for no reason but to stretch my pins / up in the window was this bird / a right cracker she was / I stopped and caught her staring down / a red lampshade that tells all I don't know why / but I was tempted by all the mysteries that glow foretold / I pretended to be staring in the shop below / transistors and electrical equipment / but up above was the socket I needed for my plug / a card said 'Sally, two flights up' / I found myself upon the stairs / grim smells and rot / knocked on the door.

SYLV *at home pouring a drink, upstage.*

SYLV: I hate to drink alone / sometimes I must / it quells the energy I have which I'd rather spend on someone / some him / or him / he leaves me with it bottled up and spare / I drown it out / my youth is going up the spout / in love that's wasted / I hate to stay in alone / how many others are like me / alone in boxes / waiting for someone or the phone to ring / what's the use to wait / and if he does / a thing of shreds and patches.

SID *and* PEARL *downstage.*

SID: So well, I knocked upon the door / and this scrubber opened
it / looking like nothing on earth / while far below it was a
mystery / I thought / she smiled / and showed a gap or three /
the rest was black / and on her face a cake of slap / one inch
thick at least / I thought I can't do this / I had my wages in
my belt / not much since times were hard / and mum needed
the gelt / for rent and clobber for the kids / a coat as well / but
even so I couldn't now turn back / I hurtled through a quick
time for . . . don't ask / it cost a bomb.

PEARL: You promised, Sid, you said I could have a new coat.

SID: And found myself outside the electrical store / and nothing to
show except a rancid shag / and wages short / felt sick and
empty / I couldn't buy my wife her winter coat / I sacrificed
my wife for that / I'm sorry Pearl, I said, I earned a few bob
less / you'll have to wait a week or two / felt real vile / she
said.

PEARL: You promised Sid / you said that I would have a new coat
Sid, this winter / that's what you said.

SID: I know / don't go on / don't start nagging / I sweat out my
guts for you / I break my balls that you should not go short.

PEARL: Don't shout in front of the kids!

SID: I sit down by a bench all day / machining trousers for five
bob / and dust choking my lungs / and the noise of the
machines / you wouldn't believe it / and fifty in a room / ten
pair of pants a day / I slog to make / cut and trim / then throw
them to Greek to finish off / and put a fly in / and at the end a
Mick to press them / I got callused hands already from the
shears / a spine that's curved forever / and a cough that can't
be cured by all the medicines in the world / that's known to
man / to make a haven for my family / which is a little
heaven / so don't get on my tits.

PEARL: OK / I'll wait / sure I can wait / wanna cuppa?

SID: I wouldn't say no to nice cuppa, Pearl.

PEARL: I hope Mike's OK / I haven't seen him since yesterday.

SID: Does that surprise you / you look surprised as if that's new /
that he appears when you see him and not before / a plague

he's been to me (*To himself*) . . . it cost a bomb.

PEARL: What did?

SID: Nothing, what did I say?

PEARL: You said it cost a bomb.

SID: Oh I was miles away.

In the café, or MIKE *walking. The following can be said either by a chorus of* LADS *or by* MIKE, *lecturing the* LADS' *still faces. For continuity,* MIKE *should be alone.*

LES: At least the joy of being strong.

STEVE: Of owning your own body.

RALPH: Your capitals, your guts.

KEN: In your hands you hold the pleasure or the pain of the Western world.

LES: Hands can be the instrument of life.

STEVE: Or death.

RALPH: What's it to be?

KEN: Either way you have to choose.

LES: You who watch and never had a choice.

STEVE: You look the only way.

RALPH: How many times did you want to lash out?

KEN: Give vent to what you felt?

LES: The bile that's choked within.

STEVE: Instead ate humble pie.

RALPH: How often did you want to impress the missus?

KEN: Be Charles Atlas and kill the dragon like St George?

LES: And how often did you tremble in your socks?

STEVE: Afraid in case you lost . . .

RALPH: Or broke a nose.

KEN: Ooh, painful.

LES: Damaged an eye even.

STEVE: There's lots to fear.

RALPH: And swallowed some offence.

KEN: A mouthful of slagging vile.

LES: And wished next day . . .

STEVE: When safe at home that you had taken chances.

RALPH: A memory to chat about on wintry nights to all the kids . . .

KEN: Of how you were a hero.

LES: For a while.

STEVE: Never mind, you made a bomb in wholesale and made a
fortune in the market like a lucky Joe.

RALPH: Beneath it all you wanted at some time to be a hero with
your dukes.

KEN: To emulate John Wayne.

LES: Or other prince of celluloid.

STEVE: Because that's your courage that you stake.

RALPH: Your guts you gamble on the street.

KEN: Opposing some hard tearaway.

LES: And whip him.

STEVE: That's worth a lot.

RALPH: You know it in your heart.

KEN: How many carry an emblem of some shame . . .

LES: Some insult not yet purged away . . .

STEVE: That gnaws your very vitals?

RALPH: You forget, you say! Ignore that cad.

KEN: Don't get mixed up with riff-raff, darling, says your dolly
bird.

LES: You jump into a cab.

STEVE: Agree with her . . . they're not worth it.

RALPH: Ignore the mob.

KEN: Yet underneath it all you wish there were a Bruce Lee
tucked away.

LES: Or a Mike.

STEVE: Instead you pour a drink and gas about an incident at
school when for a minute you stood up to wrath.

RALPH: You play the incident again.

LES: And yet again.

LES: Re-run the entire scene.

STEVE: Imagine what you would have done . . .

RALPH: Had you the chance again.

KEN: Let him say it once more, you utter in your dreams.

LES: Too late.

STEVE: And if you had the chance again . . .

RALPH: Wouldn't it have been the same?

KEN: But knights are born not made.

LES: The others stand round and watch.

(*They march off as tight group and comfort* MIKE.)

MIKE: See ya tonight then.

RALPH: Bird's in the club.

STEVE: Don't feel well, Mike.

LES: Gotta fix me scooter.

KEN: Me mother's sick.

MIKE: Don't let me down, will ya?

ALL: Course, Mike, yeah, etc.

Sylv's pad.

SYLV: What are you doing here?

MIKE: Aren't you pleased to see me / I had to see you / wish me luck / I got a little flicker in my guts / I must confess.

SYLV: Of what?

MIKE: Doubt and sick all mixed.

SYLV: Then don't go.

MIKE: Have to.

SYLV: Why?

MIKE: Sylv, the Fates have wrapped me up / to be delivered this night / I've got to go / revenge is one / strong one for a pal / as for the rest / what else is there to do / sure there is always a day that has to come / that you would much rather avoid / postpone / and send a card / forgive me / but / I can't make it this week / you lie in bed and sweat / hope the daylight never comes / it's not tomorrow any more / it's now / the readiness is all / but after if I'm still around / I'll pop on over.

SYLV: I wanted much more than that / the occasional hallo love and how are you / you busy tonight shall I come round / to sit and wait is not my idea of paradise / in case you decide this is the night that you decide to come / and what do we do but pass the time until it's time to go and 'see ya! Be in touch!' / I'd like to be there for a man / who lives for the moment / so I can live for the moment too / when we can meet / and protect that which we grow together within me / not here love – here's a ton / go get it fixed / a hundred quid to kick it out /

buy back the space I'd rather fill / a hundred quid / to kill /
that's easy for the man in love with death and pride / you are
more keen to see your Hoxton pal so you can be a tearaway /
the King of Stamford Hill / if you gave me as much as you
give him / I'd be so happy / if I obsessed you half as much /
you'll give each other all the thrills you are afraid to spill on
me / you are in love with him not me / so go enjoy yourself /
be free / far easier for a hand to make a fist than hold it open
for a caress / easier for you to smash yourself into his body
than to mine / to make yourself into a ball of hate wound up /
so you can hide yourself from what you fear / be a hard man /
'cause hard covers the soft / the soft that's underneath is what
you fear / my woman's body tells me / is soft to make things
grow / its softness breaks down your rocks / can destroy you
like water wears down stone / go to your lover Mike / go, and
don't come back / go / be alone / and who will put you
together again when you're a pile of broken bones?

MIKE: Thank you very much / I'll bear in mind all what you said /
I spit out all my angst / confess my guts / wished I had bit my
tongue first / before I let those soppy words crawl out my
gob / I had a shred or two of doubt I do confess / and that is
all no need to make a song and dance / accuse me of some
vileness in my act with you / it takes two to tango / don't
forget that / anyway I'm here aren't I / I come to you don't I /
there's no one else / at least . . . you get the best / sometimes
the worst / that's what it's all about / that's how it goes / that's
what they spout in church even / for better or for . . . / I'm
sorry you don't find me your ideal / you never will / you birds
have scored into your head / some geezer all identikit / a
mister right / but they never can and never will fit the little
pictures that you make / so without more ado / I'll take my
leave of you.

Street.

MIKE: Didn't wish me luck even! I dunno / I'm all alone, that's
how it goes / my mates have fled / left me for dead / and most
pernicious woman left me too / I need a friend / need

someone / something / just to tell it to / tell me I'm OK / I'm good / nah I don't need / anyone / I need revenge / that's something to get on with / that's a start / don't take away my *raison* dirt track / don't take away my art / I'll be myself again / but now a numbing sickness is sliding down my gut / I'll force it back / I clench my fist / it feels like jelly / like a baby's paw / if only I had the strength of a kitten I could win / I see myself reflected in a windowpane / a death's skull stares me in the face / where is my resolution / where the spleen that had me think I was the king of the master race / bearded with the sweat of fear / a demon came and sucked my blood / they sense victims and hover like bats / the filthy beasts / that's all right / who ever felt happy before a fight / you go in sick but once you start and get the first sting in / your face you then forget your problems / like an actor on the stage / scared shitless in the wings but once he's on then he's the king.

(CHORUS *rushes on – reflects* MIKE's *walk upstage.*)

OTHERS: (*At random*) You can do it, Mike.

Didn't wish me luck even.

How do you think you'll do?

He's mad to go.

No blood of mine.

But hers . . .

One minute, Mike.

LES: Hackney marshes.

(*The* CHORUS *leaves the stage.* MIKE *is alone. He acts the battle.*)

MIKE: He hits me with a hook / I'm down / a bolt to fell an ox / crumbles slow / then smashes me with a right / and now / I sway / a drunk looking for a hold / a volley a hard straight comes whipping out / smashing home / I go down slow like the *Titanic* / but grab hold on the way / and drag him down leaking red from all openings but still I hold him / close / he can't be hit / too close / and with my almighty arm I lock his neck into a vice / where do I get the strength / the brute's amazed thinking it was all done / but finds his head being smashed into the wall / but like he's made of rock / he twists himself from out my grip like some mad demented bull and snorts screams and kicks but by this time I dodge the sledge hammers and hold him at bay / alive again as if the blows have woken me from some deep sleep / I'm myself again / we move and circle / it's quiet as the grave / all tense waiting / the beast kicks out and hard / I grab a leg / and down he falls / hard / but with almighty strength the brute is up again / sneers and foams / and rams his fingers round my throat / grips hard / the others round about / screaming / kill the bastard / tear out his guts / and rip his balls off / I pull off his wrist and then we twist / fall / rolling / each trying to find a hold / and lashing out from time to time / knee / elbow / head / boot / whatever finds itself unoccupied and free for service / we break away and stand streaming like two dragons breathing flame / fighting to the death / each waiting for the other to move / still / just the sound of breath / then in the beast goes and fast and throws himself on me like to annihilate me once and for all / I go flying back thrown by the mass of hate and crash both down in a welter of struggling seething flesh / twisting foaming heaving screaming / I'm stomped on / sounds unearthly are heard / I fear it must end / and bad / he's on my chest / his fist drawn back / one horrible almighty gnarl of bone and brought it crashing down on to my face / pow and then again pow and now again pow / I can hear the sickening crunch / but I protect what how I can / draw energy from the deep and thrust my hand up underneath his jaw / with the other I smash it home / the brute stumbles / pulled off balance / my face is crimson blind by blood / I wipe with one hand / I'm upon him now spraying his blood on both like we were swimming in it / this time grip his throat and hold it fast / tight / tighter / after long time we topple over / again / rise slow like prehistoric monsters / the beast screaming / words / spitting out / no meaning / splattered curses / he bows like to pounce again / I then kick / it lands home dead square in the face / then follow up both hands working like pumps / like you never saw.

CHORUS: Pow-pow-pow-pow-pow / pow-pow-pow-pow-pow!

MIKE: But you wouldn't believe the strength of the brute / inhuman like / grinning like a gargoyle / he stands there, says come on do something / and charges again / I can't believe / as if my own powers mean nothing / see hopelessness and fear now flooding in as fast as strength is flowing out / we grip each other for a hold / to throw one or the other down / but I'm losing all belief / I'm down / as if it's better there / just lie covering my face / I'm kicked pow / once twice pow / feebly attempt to rise pow / kicked down / the fourth time in his glee / too keen, he misses / slides over on the blood slippery deck / heavy as lead / I climb up in agony / but do not miss the chance / to connect the monster's head with a bone-shattering well-aimed knee / it stops him dead / it looks surprised / astonished / and for luck / throw all my weight into a right which crashes open all in his skull / out go the lights pow / the Hoxton King keeled over / toppled / crashed down / in one terrible long rasping blood gurgled moan / then it was over / he twitched / raised his head / spewed between his bloody teeth the words / 'Nice one' / then lay quite still / me yelling / the lads about looked sick and pale / were shattered in their souls / and thought the future black / I wiped the blood away / put on my coat / they parted quickly from me when I left / I staggered into casualty at London Hospital who fixed me up.

Gang as group like cheerleaders. They trot around the stage to give him a hero's welcome.

MATES: Well done and welcome home / you done us proud / terrific / so we heard.

KEN: Report was trumps.

RALPH: From far and wide.

LES: Your triumphs sung to the four corners of the manor.

STEVE: You look a mess.

ALL: But hold your head up / you're the ace.

MIKE: Oh yeah / my nose is broke / my lovely profile's gone.

RALPH: You'll get it back.

STEVE: You'll look better than ever once it heals.

KEN: Don't you fear.

LES: Sensational it were, I swear.

RALPH: My heart was out there for you . . .

STEVE: Stomping in my chest . . .

KEN: Like fifty insane drummers.

LES: When you got up and curled your right . . .

RALPH: I said a little prayer for its journey into space.

ALL: He didn't know what year it was / he didn't care!

MIKE: So where were you, deserted me ye men of little faith / all mouth and trousers when it comes down to the crunch / you could have shown a face at least to plonk your minces on the scene should tricky business raise its ugly face / instead you wait for news of my impending fate / it's over now / it's done / so what's it all about / I've had enough of this / I'm out.

MIKE *creeps into his house – enters Pearl's and Sid's room for the first time.*

MIKE: Hallo.

SID: What the . . .? Look at your face.

PEARL: Mike, oh God, what happened to you?

MIKE: I had a fight . . . but I won . . . I did it.

SID: So, look at you, what do you want / a medal?

MIKE: No / I just wanted to tell you / it's the last one I'll have.

SID: So tell me something new.

PEARL: Leave him, Sid.

SID: He's proud / he comes in here to tell us he's proud.

MIKE: It was hard / yeah I'm proud / his gang did up little Harry.

SID: Don't give us this talk / this time of night / your gang warfare / a gangster I've got and he comes in yet like he's a hero.

MIKE: I just wanted to talk to you.

SID: So / you've talked.

MIKE: I needed to tell someone.

SID: So you've told me / what do you want us to do?

MIKE: Nothing, just nothing you miserable lump of complaint / that's all you've done all your life / what else are you good for / nothing / and you give nothing / I've listened to your miserable snivelling complaints for years / I've had enough of you / a swollen bag of useless opinions like all the old sods like you.

PEARL: Don't aggravate your father / his ulcer's killing him / go to bed / wash your face and go to bed / you don't look well, son.

MIKE: Ma / you've tied yourself to a lump of concrete / and it's sinking into the swamp.

PEARL: And who's complaining?

MIKE: I am!

PEARL: Don't worry about me / go to bed.

MIKE: OK.

(MIKE *exits*.)

SID: Tell him in the morning to go / he's got to go / I for one can't take any more / so tell him / Pearl he's our son / but he's got to get out of this house / I can't take any more of it.

PEARL: I'll tell him.

SID: Make sure you do.

PEARL: I will / I said I will.

SID: He's got to go somewhere and do something / but I don't want him around any more / I'm sorry.

PEARL: In the morning I'll tell him to go.

SID: Don't soften up and change your mind.

PEARL: I'll tell him it's best for all of us if he went.

SID: KEN: You'll tell him that.

PEARL: Yeah.

SID: 'Cause this can't go on like this.

PEARL: I know that.

SID: Then we can have a bit of peace in our old age.

PEARL: Yeah.

SID: You know what I mean.

PEARL: Of course / I'll tell him in the morning / I'll tell him he must find somewhere else to live and not come back this time.

SID: I did my best.

PEARL: Yeah.

SID: Didn't I? . . . You sound as if I didn't well / didn't I or not / did I show him those ways?

PEARL: No, I did.

SID: What you talking about?

PEARL: From me he saw that not to fight was to give in / he saw that I never fought back / so he had to.

SID: You'll tell him in the morning to go!

Epilogue.

MIKE: I can't go on like this / look at me / my nose is out of joint / I can't see straight / I've got no job to speak of but I won / I won / I beat the beast / with my own two hands alone / I reached out and defeated what they feared / I conquered my own doubts when sick inside / that's great / so tell me where to go and what to do / and what's the trick that makes for happy days and nights / the fireside and mates around for Xmas / the wife cooking a bird / a baby going gaga / the colour telly on / the Daimler shining round the front / what did you do to get it / do you thieve / stay on at school / or work your loaf / inherit some cosy chunk of loot from papa / go on tell me the trick / what's the clue I need to know some answers / or I'll make my own / you who sit comfortably at home / who wake up with a grin and toast and eggs / tell me what you do and how you do it / never mind I'll find out / I'll get the wind on you / I'll break out of this maze / and sniff around your pen / I'll be the beast you fear / until I get an answer / straight up I will / you had me do your dirt / and stood around to gape / while I put down the fears that kept you sleepless in your beds / there'll come another beast / for every one you kill / there will grow another head.

Further epilogue.

PEARL *and* SID. GANG *as respectable people stand behind them.*

SID: Don't you worry / we did what we could / he's not so bad / a little wild / but soon he'll find his head / and if he don't / well then / others will help / there are the courts / police and magistrates to guide him on the way / prisons to help persuade / and keep society safe / so all in all he's no real threat to you and me / we keep our noses clean / pay the rent

and rates / smile our social smile / and leave when they call
time.

PEARL: But he's your son.

SID: No son of mine.

Blackout.
Faces of characters.

GREEK

CHARACTERS

EDDY
DAD
WIFE
MUM
FORTUNE-TELLER
MANAGER OF CAFE
DOREEN
SPHINX
WAITRESS 1
WAITRESS 2

AUTHOR'S NOTE

Greek came to me via Sophocles, trickling its way down the millenia until it reached the unimaginable wastelands of Tufnell Park – a land more fantasized than real, being an amalgam of the deadening war zones that some areas of London had become. Tufnell Park was just a word to play with – like our low comedians play with the sound of East Cheam for example – so no real offence to the inhabitants.

In my eyes, Britain seemed to have become a gradually decaying island, preyed upon by the wandering hordes who saw no future for themselves in a society which had few ideals or messages to offer them. The violence that streamed through the streets, like an all-pervading effluence, the hideous Saturday night fever as the pubs belched out their dreary occupants, the killing and maiming at public sports, plus the casual slaughtering of political opponents in Northern Ireland, bespoke a society in which an emotional plague had taken root. It was a cold place in my recollection, lit up from time to time by the roar of the beast – the beast of frustration and anger, whose hunger is appeased by these revolving scraps, which momentarily dull its needs. We were the world's greatest video watchers, since we had lost the ability to speak to each other. We sat like zombies, strangled in our attempts to communicate, feeding off the flickering tube like patients wired to support systems.

Oedipus found a city in the grip of a plague and sought to rid the city of its evil centre represented by the Sphinx. Eddy seeks to reaffirm his beliefs and inculcate a new order of things with his vision and life-affirming energy. His passion for life is inspired by the love he feels for his woman, and his detestation of the degrading environment he inherited. If Eddy is a warrior who holds up the smoking sword as he goes in, attacking all that he finds polluted, at the same time he is at heart an ordinary young man with whom many I know will find identification. The play is also a love story.

In writing my 'modern' *Oedipus* it wasn't too difficult to find contemporary parallels, but when I came to the 'blinding' I paused, since in my version it wouldn't have made sense, given Eddy's non-fatalistic disposition, to have him embark on such an act of self-hatred – unless I slavishly aped the original. One day a friend gave me a book to read which provided an illumination to my problem in an almost identical situation. The book is called *Seven Arrows* by Hyemeyohsts Storm. It contains a passage of such tenderness and simplicity that I was immediately given the key to my own ending:

'How is it, Hawk,' I asked him, 'that I should not make love to Sweet Water, my mother?'

'Do you love her?' he asked me.

I answered, 'Yes, more than anyone else . . . But . . . children of such a love are born wrong.'

'Have you ever seen one of these children?' asked Night Bear.

'No, I have not. And I have never known anyone who has.' . . .

'Then it is like everything else . . . It seems an easy thing to hear when a son kills someone, even his mother, but it is hard on people's ears when they hear of a son loving his mother.'

Greek was first performed at the Half Moon Theatre, London, on 11 February 1980. The cast was as follows:

EDDY and FORTUNE-TELLER	Barry Philips
DAD and MANAGER OF CAFE	Matthew Scurfield
WIFE, DOREEN, and WAITRESS 1	Linda Marlowe
MUM, SPHINX, and WAITRESS 2	Janet Amsden
Director	Steven Berkoff

Greek was transferred to the Arts Theatre Club, London, in September 1980. The cast was as follows:

EDDY and FORTUNE-TELLER	Barry Philips
DAD and MANAGER OF CAFE	Matthew Scurfield
WIFE, DOREEN, and WAITRESS 1	Linda Marlowe
MUM, SPHINX, and WAITRESS 2	Deirdre Morris
Director	Steven Berkoff

A new production of *Greek* was presented at Wyndham's Theatre, London, on 29 June 1988. The cast was as follows:

EDDY and FORTUNE-TELLER	Bruce Payne
DAD and MANAGER OF CAFE	Steven Berkoff
WIFE, DOREEN, and WAITRESS 1	Gillian Eaton
MUM, SPHINX, and WAITRESS 2	Georgia Brown
Director	Steven Berkoff

Place: England
Time: present
Stage setting: kitchen table and four simple chairs. These will
    function in a number of ways. They can be everything one
    wants them to be from the platform for the SPHINX to the
    café. They also function as the train; the environment which
    suggests EDDY's humble origins becoming his expensive and
    elaborate home in Act Two. The table and chairs merely
    define spaces and act as an anchor or base for the actors to
    spring from. All other artifacts are mimed or suggested. The
    walls are three square upright white panels, very clinical and
    at the same time indicating Greek classicism. The faces are
    painted white and are clearly defined. Movement should be
    sharp and dynamic, exaggerated and sometimes bearing the
    quality of seaside cartoons. The family act as a chorus for all
    other characters and environments.

ACT ONE

SCENE I

EDDY: So, I was spawned in Tufnell Park that's no more than a
stone's throw from the Angel / a monkey's fart from
Tottenham or a bolt of phlegm from Stamford Hill / it's a
cesspit, right . . . a scum-hole dense with the drabs who prop
up corner pubs, the kind of pub where ye old arse-holes
assemble . . . the boring turds who save for Xmas with clubs
. . . my mum did that . . . save all year for her slaggy Xmas
party of boozy old relatives in Marks and Sparks' cardigans
who stand all year doing as little as they can while they had
one hand in the boss's till and the other scratching their balls
. . . they'd all come over and vomit up Guinness and mum's
unspeakable excuse for cuisine all over the bathroom, adjust
their dentures . . . rage against the blacks, envying their
cocks, loathe the yids, envying their gelt . . . hate everything
under thirty that walks and fall asleep in front of the telly . . .
so they'd gather in the pubs, usually a smelly corner pub run
by a rancid thick-as-pig-shit paddy who sold nothing but
booze and crisps in various chemical flavours to their yokel
patrons who played incessant games of cruddy darts, drink
yards of stale gnat's piss beer and chatter like . . .

DAD: See Arsenal last week? . . .

DOREEN: I think England's team's all washed up . . .

MUM: What abaht the way he dribbled the . . .

DAD: Nah nah, he's lorst his bottle . . .

DOREEN: Do leave orf . . .

EDDY: The stink of the pub rises and the OAPs sit in the corner
staring out into the dreams they never had with a drip of snot
hanging off the ends of their noses and try to make a pint last
four hours . . . start crowding up now and the paddy starts
raving fucking 'time' and pulling the glass out of your hand

while he's bursting your eardrums screaming like a sergeant-major, his wife attempts to shovel some paint on her evil hate-all face which looks as if it's been applied by a drunken epileptic on a roller coaster . . .

MUM (*as chorus*): 'Allo luv.

EDDY: She foams . . . staring out of a yellow face with little snot-brown eyes like two raisins in a plate of porridge. And if by chance you lean over the bar too far some bastard monster cunt Alsatian leaps at you, its dripping fangs simply dying to rip your fucking throat out . . . so I gave up going to the corner pub with its late night chorus of lurchy . . .

FAMILY (*as chorus*): G'night.

EDDY: . . . and . . .

FAMILY (*as chorus*): See ya, Tel.

EDDY: We got wine bars now, handsome. That's much better – sit down, a half bottle of château or Bollinger, some pâté and salad by a chick who looks as if she's been fresh frozen . . . you take your favourite woman there, my woman very nice mate, looks like she's been just minted and sharp as new mown grass, knickers as white as Xmas, eyes like the bluest diamonds . . . a pair of fiery red rubies for lips, the light hits them and shatters your eyes, she smiles and your heart leaps into your throat and you carry a demon between your thighs and up to your chin . . . the whole time . . . I wear shades to protect myself against the brightness of her teeth . . . no tobacco stains on them boy . . . breath like an ocean breeze on Brighton Pier . . . now could you take her to that pub? Could you ever! Nah! It's really for the old fascists singing war songs on the pavement and . . .

FAMILY: Knees up Mother Brown . . .
Knees up Mother Brown . . .

EDDY: So I go to my wine bar with the bird who's carved out of onyx and marble and laced in the smells of the promise of sex the way you wouldn't believe . . . I swim in her like I was plunging into the Jordan for a baptism. So anyway one day my dad calls me in the kitchen.

DAD: Come in son . . .

EDDY: He says,

DAD: . . . I wanna chat to ya, or we could go down the corner to the pub, I'll buy you a drink.

EDDY: 'No! Not that pub,' I yelp in real and unfeigned terror. 'I'll throw some tea into a pot instead' . . . mum's out . . . the *Daily Mirror* crossword half finished . . . well it is a bit grotty but homely in a sickly sort of way if you're not used to anything better, it's not like the interior of a Zen temple but cosy. A few crumbs on the carpet, some evil photos of my sister on the mantelpiece and a picture of granny looking like Mussolini in drag which they all looked like in those far off days of pre-history, the poodle's shit again behind the cocktail cabinet . . . the old bacon rinds sit stinking in the pan and the room renches of lard. I made dad a cuppa. Mum's at bingo and sis is meditating in the bedroom on the squeezing out of some juicy blackheads . . . her old knickers lie sunny side up . . . she always left them on the floor for mum to scoop up while I wouldn't have touched them except with those pincers that pick up radium behind thick walls. So we sit down and he confesses this story to me . . . pulls out a fag and sits there with his flies half undone, and the ash of his fag ready to drop all over his shirt. I try not to look at him or his flies. I try to occupy my thoughts with my latest Stan Kenton. I look out of the window and see the grey clouds of Tottenham stray across the window pane . . . a tiny sliver of sun is struggling to peep through, sees what it has to shine on and thinks 'fuck it – is it worth it' and beats a retreat. So dad says . . .

DAD: Look here son . . .

EDDY: I says 'yes dad' clocking his work-raped face, his tasteless shit-heap Burton ready-made trousers and his deadly drip-dry shirt that acquires BO faster than shit attract flies . . . I clock all this fusion of rubbish and say 'yes, dad? what do you want to chat abaht', never hearing much else out of his gob than . . .

DAD: Send the darkies back to the jungle . . .

EDDY: . . . and . . .

DAD: ''Itler got the trains running on time' . . .

EDDY: You got a lot of Nazi lovers among the British down and
out. Lazy bastards wondered why at the end of a life of
skiving and strikes Moisha down the road copped a few bob
or why the Cypriots had a big store full of goodies not that
pathetic shit-heap down our street that flogs only Mother's
Pride mousetrap cheese and a few miserable tins of pilchards
and Heinz baked beans and a dreary cunt inside saying, 'no,
we don't get no demand for that' when asked for something
only slightly more exotic than Kelloggs. So dad did not come
out with any of that fascist bullshit which relieved me since
the Front were full of dads like this and that cunt in the
grocery ship . . . 'yeah dad' I said 'what's on your bonce' . . .
his face squeezed up like it's hard to say, like those old ads
for Idris lemon squash showed a screwed-up lemon and
comes out with . . .

SCENE 2

DAD: When you were a nipper / we went to a gypsy, a fortune
teller / bit of a giggle / an Easter fair / don't laugh / a caper,
what else / spent a tosheroon on a bit of a thrill, don't talk to
me about thrills / so in we went / the gypsy asks 'have I a
son?' 'I have' I says, I mean who don't have a son? His face
meanwhile staring into the ball / his eyes all popping / I'm
not taking it for gen, straight up, a lark / Easter and all / I've
got a lovely bunch and all that / his face gets all contorted and
twisted and he says / he sees a violent death for this son's
father / do what! but I'm his dad / come orf it / don't get all
dramatic / we get on like houses blazing / 'and I see' he says,
'something worse than death / and that's a bunk-up with his
mum' / 'I'll give you a backhand' I utter / 'you're having me
on / you been smoking them African Woodbines' / 'No' he
shrieks, 'I see it, and what I see I see / so don't pay me, just
scarper / leave my tent / keep your gelt' / outside we ran, your
mum was white as Persil / I as yellow as a Chinaman with

jaundice / course we took no notice / forgot about it like, but
not quite / waited till you got to be a bloke and then one day I
said 'Dinah / you remember that darkie in the fair who came
out with all that filth about Eddy', one morning in bed just
lying there, redigesting bits of past and sucking still the
flavour of some juicy memories /

MUM: Not many . . .

DAD: Our Dinah slurps . . .

MUM: Not many, I nearly dropped Doreen with whom I was six
months' pregnant then / funny times.

DAD: 'Well' I say, 'that fair is back in town, the same firm fifteen
years later / let's bowl down and see that geezer, tell that
Hornsey gypsy what a lot of old bollocks / how he upset my
missus with his pack of dirty lies / so off we went / doubted
somehow that he'd still be there, since he was pushing sixty
then / you never know, we waited our turn / it was the same
name 'Have your future read / Fantoni's magic crystal
gazer' / shall we go in? . . .

MUM: Do you think we should? . . .

DAD: Why not, it's now or never / we went pale a bit but in we
marched / same old schmutter on the table, the beads we
walked through and the bit of old glass and no, it weren't
him, so I said 'Where's the old geezer that we once saw
whose handle now you seem to have?'

EDDY (as the 'GYPSY'): My late old man . . .

DAD: He said . . .

EDDY (as the 'GYPSY'): Five years ago he uttered his last / and fell
off the perch / but taught me the trade / imbued his vision in
me / I got his powers now / so don't you fret / if he did good
by you / donate a quid and I'll do my best . . .

DAD: So Ed, your mum and I sat down just like before, the years
they shrank away / just like a hole fell out of the earth and
time and space had faded away / we seemed then to have
hurtled back those fifteen years / in that small tent / the
music tinkling through from the carousel outside and that
funny smell / the shouts growing faint, just the whiff of stale
grass under our feet / and like the tent seemed small / like a

trap and suddenly hot and nothing outside just quiet but his
face / his face getting all twisted up just like his dad / his
mouth all white and tight like an earthquake was going on
inside his nut and his lips were straining against it coming
out. Dinah sussed but natch we waited / 'don't tell me' I said,
'you see a son of mine' / his eyes looked up, affirmed / no
word, just that look and his tight mouth / like holding back
something worse than vomit / 'and you see something worse',
I says, 'like a nasty accident perhaps' / He nodded, parted his
lips enough to mouth the word 'death' which he hadn't the
guts to sound. He then stared hard at Dinah / but we had
enough and wanted not to hear the other half but fled / I
turned and snatched the quid back from the table / I don't
know why / but like before when I got my money back / it
seemed to say by taking back the gelt that it couldn't
happen / his eyes looked like pity / like those sweet pics you
get in Woolie's of those kids with a tear just ripe to drop / I
know it's just a funfair Ed / a laugh, a bit of a giggle / I didn't
blame the kid / what do you make of it son / you don't fancy
your old mum do you son! You don't want to kill me do you
boy?

DOREEN: Leave off you two.

EDDY: Doreen! His face hung there like a soggy worn-out
testicle / mouth open and eyes like carrier bags / fancy my
mum! I could sooner go down on Hitler, than do anything
my old man so gravely feared / no dad / but all this aggro and
old wives' tale gone and put you in a tiz / I'll leave home /
split and scarper / the Central Line goes far these days and
that's to foreign climes / I'll piss off tomorrow / I needed to
escape this cruddy flat and this excuse seemed good as any /
tata ma and pa. They waved to me outside the flats . . . my
mum looked sad / her spotty apron wrapped round her like
the flag of womanhood / I never saw her out of it / always
standing in the kitchen like some darkie slave behind dad
and me and sis . . .

DAD: Bung us the toast.

EDDY: Where's the jam?

DOREEN: Pig!

MUM: More tea love?

DAD: Bung us the toast.

EDDY: Where's the jam?

DOREEN: Pig!

MUM: More 'taters love?

DOREEN: I'm on a diet.

MUM: More cake love?

EDDY: No mum, I've had six slices already.

MUM: Go on have some more.

EDDY: I don't want no more, you rancid old boot.

DAD: Hey!

EDDY: I'd spray affectionately.

MUM: Oh he don't like my cake.

EDDY: She'd simper . . . 'all right bung us another slice and I'll
    wedge it down wiv a mug of tea to slop it up a bit.'

DAD: Bung us the toast.

EDDY: Where's the jam?

DOREEN: Pig!

MUM: More tea love?

EDDY: She gazes at us with moist eyes on all of us slurping like fat
    pigs in a trough / we'd leave a wreck filled table, ma's
    washing up, how well she knew that washtop / dad's picking
    out losers in the worn out armchair / sis is fitting in her cap
    for the night's activity cussing and swearing in the next room
    as she struggles with it . . .

DOREEN: Fuck it!

EDDY: And mum sits in front of the box watching some dozy
    cretin making cunts out of the cunts who go on to win a few
    bob / mum's giggling in her glee / her legs like a patchwork
    quilt from hogging the electric fire, while I was in my little
    room plotting and dreaming of ruling the world / take a
    Charles Atlas course / wondering if the Queen gets it often /
    or planning a dose of robbery with violets or glorious bodily
    charm / so in my little room I plotted, smoked / played Stan
    Kenton and wanked wiv mum's cooking oil. Now no more
    will I escape to my little domain . . . hearing the sounds of

hughie phlegm in the next room through the snot-encrusted walls. So all in a flash these thoughts slinked like maggots through my bonce as I waved my goodbyes to the fast-diminishing figures of my mum and dad wed together in the distance like mould on cheese . . . my dad was the mould / never mad about him . . . as I reached the end of the road I could only see the apron and lost the figure / the apron stayed in my mind the longest. When my old lady went to the happy hunting ground I would frame that apron.

MUM: Take good care of yourself.

DAD: Don't forget to write.

DOREEN: Got your photo.

MUM: Be a good boy.

DAD: Send us some money.

DOREEN: Miss yer.

MUM: Love yer Ed.

DAD: Take care on the roads.

DOREEN: Au revoir.

MUM: 'Bye, boy . . .

SCENE 3

DAD: The toast is burnt.

MUM: Saw Vi the other day.

DAD: Neighbours don't complain no more.

MUM: Matilda's had six kittens.

DAD: Where's my smokes?

MUM: 'Ere, 'ave you seen the cooking oil?

DAD: I miss our little Ed.

MUM: How will he fare, strikes up and down the country.

DAD: The City sits in a heap of shit.

MUM: Of uncollected garbage everywhere.

DAD: The heatwaves turn it all to slime and filthy germs hang thickly in the air / the rats are on the march.

MUM: Transport sits idly at the docks where workers slink around and for a hefty bribe may let you have your avocado

or Dutch cabbage . . . petrol's obsolete as thousands of
rusting cars lie swelling up our streets to vital services like
ambulances which take a month to get from place to place.

DAD: The country's in a state of plague / while parties of all shades
battle for power to sort the shit from the shinola / the
Marxists and the Workers' party call for violence to put an
end to violence and likewise the wankers suggest hard
solutions like thick chains and metal toecaps / poisoned darts
half-inched from local taverns / anyone who wants to kill,
maim and destroy / arson, murder and hack are being
recruited for the new revolutionary party / the fag libs are
holding violent demos to be able to give head in the public
park when the garbage strike is over and not to be persecuted
for screwing on the top deck of buses.

MUM: Forte's catering is resisting the staff's demand to be paid
wages and is recruiting workers from the jungles of South
America.

DAD: Yet also strongly resisting the need to clear out the rats for
which they are duly famous.

MUM: Most of the stores are closed but Fortnum's and Harrods
soldier on shrilly packed with screaming advocates of limited
nuclear drop on Hyde Park and so rid the country they say of
a twisted bunch of rancid and perverted filth.

DAD: The nights in Hyde Park are lit by fires and the sound of
tom toms from the Brixton Black Workers Revolutionary
Gay Lib joins forces with White Is Ugly Forced Abortion /
wanking is not a town in China but an alternative to the
Filthy Men Female Party Group.

MUM: Meanwhile the rats head down Edgware Road up to
Oxford Street preparing to turn right into Bond Street / get
down Piccadilly and raid Fortnum's, pick up their mates at
Forte's and join forces to make all resistance impossible
seeing how all resistance is locked in internecine strife.

DAD: The rats march across Piccadilly avoiding Soho where the
food is dangerous even for rats, heading down to the Strand,
collect the Savoy contingent, overfat rats, not sleek for battle
but just good germ carriers with rotten teeth, head across

Waterloo Bridge and the National Theatre . . . try to wake the theatre rats who have been long in coma from a deadly attack of nightly brainwash.

MUM: Those that can be woken will begin the number two division and streak up Drury Lane to Holborn and on to King's Cross . . .

DAD: Avoiding the carcasses of rotting football Scots swollen and putrefying on the streets / those who failed to make the train and died while waiting for the next one / their flesh is deadly / the rats come marching in.

MUM: Maggot is our only hope, love.

DAD: If we only had more maggots to eat through the stinking woodpile. But how is poor Ed going to manage in all this? . . .

SCENE 4

EDDY: The shit has hit the fan as if from a great height / I walked and walked / the sirens like wailing banshees from black marias tear along the garbage-filled London street, chock full of close-shaved men in blue and clubs in black / stacked full of teeth hate-clenched / wiv fists all hungry for their daily exercise . . . the Scotties line the kerb face down in vomit which swishes down the rat-infested gutters . . . dumb jocks down for their dozy game of football / some excuse to flee their fat and shit-heap Marys in the tenements / they wear funny little hats with bobbles on and rotten teeth, they belch into the carbon air their rotgut fumes and sing a lurchy tune or two about owning some pox-ridden scab-heap called Glasgow when they don't own a pot to piss in. Then one blue-eyed bobby lays a skull or five (well aimed, son) wide open.

FAMILY: SMASH . . . SPLATTER . . . CLOBBER

EDDY: Take that you tartan git . . .

FAMILY: CRASH . . . SHATTER . . .

EDDY: Lovely . . . 'ere you, wot the fuck you doing . . . shut up . . .

FAMILY: KERACKKKK!!!!

EDDY: The whores descend and drain their filthy wallets, with their con of fuck and as the jock steps inside for fantasies of London pussy. KERACK! A villain hard-faced doth distribute a bit of sense with bars of iron / so on they go, the foul ignoble mob / they watch the match the wrong way round so pissed as newts and then they stagger into Euston Station driven by a blind sense of instinct or smell to join their follow tartans on their journey back. 'Ay, 'ad a loovely taime'. Meanwhile and spewing up the Mall down which I walked to escape the deadly gas from ten-day haggis freshly heaved upon our silver London streets. When what do I espy but fuck and shit Macdougal and his paddies from Belfast and raring to blow up anything that moves. Thick-eared, with hands like bunches of bananas / their voices from afar were like a pack of baying hounds.

FAMILY: Hate, hate, throw the bomb.
Hate, hate, throw the bomb.
(*continue low chant*)

EDDY: They were an army dressed in blue serge suits and without exception pale blue eyes and liquid gelignite stuffed in their macs and little bombs in innocent sandwich bags . . . armpits concealing stinking sweaty guns ready to blow some mother's son's head off and spray the dusty Strand with thick rich ruby / knock off some chick who God forbid could be some sweet of mine / or take the legs off some poor cunt who happened to be hanging about / and then they get all stinking in their pubs and roar with leprechaunish glee . . .

MUM (*as Irish Woman*): I've only got six Guinnesses . . .

EDDY: And fight to say who was the one to toss the bomb . . .

DOREEN (*as Irish Woman*): Whose round is it now? . . .

EDDY: How many tommies did you spray apart?

MUM (*as Irish Woman*): My fucking husband's in the pub again . . .

EDDY: How many boys were drowning in their blood / who that very night had kissed the loving girls farewell . . .

DOREEN (*as Irish Woman*): Jesus, Mary and Joseph . . .

EDDY: How many mothers' daughters copped a face of shrapnel / lost an eye . . .

DOREEN (*as Irish Woman*): Fuck my fucking husband, fuck it! / . . .

EDDY: How many mothers douse the graves of kids of eighteen /
wives and widows chatting to a piece of earth while you, you
crock of gonorrhoea in serge, wolf back another gallon, leer
home to your Bridget alone and waiting with six kids and
unwashed climb aboard dragging across her fleshy wastes
your skimpy shred of dirty prick / poke it about a bit and come
your drip of watery spunk ten seconds later / she's lying there
like a bloated cow / never known what coming is / only read
about those soft explosions in the groin / heard rumours like /
the only explosions Paddy here can make are the ones that
make you scream in fucking agony and pain awash in blood
not ecstasy and spunk. What a fucking obscenity that is . . .

DOREEN (*as Irish Woman*): FUCK FUCK FUCK AND SHIT /
MY FUCKING HUSBAND'S LYING ACROSS THE
ROAD / HIS LEGS ON ONE SIDE AND HIS
TORSO ON THE OTHER. OH GOD HELP ME . . .

EDDY: OH, MAGGOT SCRATCHER HANG THE
CUNTS / HANG THEM SLOW AND LET ME
TAKE A SKEWER AND JAB THEIR EYES OUT /
LOVELY / GREEK STYLE. . .

Hanging's no answer to the plague madam / you'd be
hanging every day / I'm human like us all / we're all the
same, linked / if you kick one his scream will hit my ears and
hurt my mind to think of some poor cunt in shtuck / the way
a kitten crying in the night will make you crawl out of your
soft pit, say what the fuck's up little moggie / free Guinness,
that's the answer and sex instruction initiated by luscious
English birds well trained in fuck and suck, then instead of
marching down the street with weapons of war and little
people on the side waving flags / they'll march down with
cocks at full alert and straining proud and strong / and
promptly get arrested. Still you can't help it / you're
drowned in aggro since a kid and dad has fed between your
flappy lugs not love but hate / has fed the history of ye olde
past to give you causes / something to do at night / has woven
a tapestry of woe inflicted on him from the distant foggy

patch called past. So what else can you do / your tired soggy
brain awash with Guinness laced with hate . . . I jumped into
the bushes and watched the curly mob in a storm of dust go
past . . . the palace was on alert . . . the sturdy chiselled
chins, fresh shaved, of our fine and brave John English ready
to defend the Queen and all her minions who represent all
that is fine in this drab of grey / this septic isle . . .

EDDY (*Sings*): Rule Britannia, Britannia rule the waves, [etc.]
Two rhythms battling for ascendancy.

FAMILY: Hate, hate, throw the bomb . . .

EDDY: Eventually got on a train / found one whose carriage wasn't
entirely smashed and wrecked and rode in peace to London's
airport Skidrow, alone and reflective in my thoughts except
for some Paki in the carriage getting a right kicking for some
no doubt vile offence like inadvertently catching the eye of
some right gallant son of Tottenham, the kicking lent a
rhythmic ritual to my thoughts which were beginning to get
formed to take some mighty fine decisions that would shoot
me on my path to riches and success, sweet-smelling pussy
and golden arms and lashing tongues. I fell into a kind of
reverie . . . I fell asleep and dreamed . . . I saw a dozen
pussies on a bed nestled between some soft and squeezy
thighs, like little gentle kittens suckling on a mother's teat /
their sweet and ivory columns hanging loosely fell apart
revealing flowers in a garden that you water and like a randy
bee I buzzed from one to t'other / their petals gently opened
wide / sent forth their perfumes in the air / and as I left they'd
close again / and then the next and each one subtly different /
each like precious luscious plants / each like a grasping
toothless mouth, hungry like open beaks of little birds while
I, like mother, into their open throats would drop my worm
which hungrily and devouringly they'd grasp. Then I
awoke / and rudely saw the world just as it is and started on
my adventures, thrust all young and sweet into the seething
heaving heap of world in which I was just a little dot. I
arrived at Heathrow, gateway to the world.

FAMILY (*as chorus of airport sounds and noises*): All this confused

me / who needs to go / do I, do you, do he / I decided to stay
and see my own sweet land / amend the woes of my own fair
state / why split and scarper like ships leaving a sinking rat / I
saw myself as king of the western world / but since I needed
some refreshment for my trials ahead, I ventured into this
little café / everywhere I looked . . . I witnessed this evidence
. . . of the British plague.

SCENE 5

FAMILY *as waiters and kitchen/café menu sounds and phrases – in
rhythm*:

VOICE 1: Soggy chips.

VOICE 2: Beans on toast. } (*Repeated as they trundle round café*).

VOICE 3: Greasy eggs.

EDDY: One coffee please and croissant and butter.

WAITRESS: Right. Cream?

EDDY: Please. Where is the butter so I might spread it lavishly
and feel its oily smoothness cover the edges of the croissant?

WAITRESS: Ain't got none. There's a plague on.

EDDY: Then why serve me the croissant knowing you had no
butter?

WAITRESS: I'll get you something else.

EDDY: I'll have a cheesecake, what's it like?

WAITRESS: Our cheescakes are all made from the nectar of the
gods mixed with the dextrous fingers of a hundred virgins
who have been whipped with bull rushes grown by the banks
of the Ganges.

EDDY: OK. I'll have one.

(*She brings it*)

. . . I've finished the coffee now and won't have any liquid to
wash the cake down with.

WAITRESS: Do you want another coffee?

EDDY: Not want but must not want but have to / you took so long
to bring the cake that I finished the coffee so bring
another . . .

WAITRESS: OK.

EDDY: But bring it before I finish the cheesecake or I'll have nothing to eat with my second cup which I only really want as a masher for the cheescake.

WAITRESS: OK. (*To another waitress*) . . . so he came all over your dress . . .

WAITRESS 2: Yeah.

WAITRESS: Dirty bastard.

WAITRESS 2: It was all thick and stringy it took ages to get off / he was sucking me like a madman when my mum walked in.

WAITRESS: No! What did she say?

WAITRESS 2: Don't forget to do behind her ears / she always forgets that.

WAITRESS: I wish my mum was understanding like that / I haven't sucked a juicy cock for ages, have you?

WAITRESS 2: No, not really, not a big horny stiff thick hot pink one.

WAITRESS: What's the biggest you've ever had?

WAITRESS 2: Ten inches.

WAITRESS: No!

WAITRESS 2: Yeah, it was all gnarled like an oak with a great big knob on the end.

WAITRESS: Yeah?

WAITRESS 2: And when it came, it shot out so much I could have wallpapered the dining room.

EDDY: Where's my fucking coffee? I've nearly finished the cheesecake and then my whole purpose in life at this particular moment in time will be lost / I'll be drinking hot coffee with nothing to wash it down with.

WAITRESS: Here you are, sorry I forgot you!

EDDY: About fucking time!

WAITRESS: Oh shut your mouth, you complaining heap of rat's shit.

EDDY: I'll come in your eyeballs you putrefying place of army gang bang.

WAITRESS: You couldn't raise a gallop if I plastered my pussy all over your face, you impotent pooftah bum boy and turd bandit.

MANAGER: (*Her husband*) What's the matter, that you raise your voice you punk and scum / fuck off!

EDDY: No one talks to me like that.

MANAGER: I just did.

EDDY: I'll erase you from the face of the earth.

MANAGER: I'll cook you in a pie and serve you up for dessert.

EDDY: I'll tear you all to pieces, rip out your arms and legs and feed them to the pigs.

MANAGER: I'll kick you to death and trample all over you / stab you with carving knives and skin you alive.
  (*They mime fight.*)

EDDY: Hit   hurt   crunch   pain   stab   jab

MANAGER: Smash   hate   rip   tear   asunder   render

EDDY: Numb   jagged   glass   gouge   out

MANAGER: Chair   breakhead   split   fist   splatter   splosh   crash

EDDY: Explode   scream   fury   strength   overpower   overcome

MANAGER: Cunt   shit   filth   remorse   weakling   blood   soaked

EDDY: Haemorrhage, rupture and swell. Split and cracklock jawsprung and neck break

MANAGER: Cave-in   rib splinter   oh the agony   the shrewd icepick

EDDY: Testicles torn out   eyes gouged and pulled   strings snapped   socket   nail   scrapped

MANAGER: Bite   swallow   suck   pull

EDDY: More smash and more power

MANAGER: Weaker and weaker

EDDY: Stronger and stronger

MANAGER: Weak

EDDY: Power

MANAGER: Dying

EDDY: Victor

MANAGER: That's it

EDDY: Tada.

WAITRESS: You killed him / I never realized words can kill.

EDDY: So can looks.

WAITRESS: You killed him / he was my husband.

EDDY: I didn't intend to I swear I didn't / he died of shock.

WAITRESS: He was a good man, solid except in his cock but he
was good to me, and now I am alone / who will I have to care
for now. Who to wait for at night while he cleans up our café
or while he's at the sauna getting relief / who to cook for or
brush the dandruff from his coat and the grease from his hat
or the tramlines from his knickers / who to comfort in the
long nights / as he worries about me / who will put the kids to
bed with a gentle cuff as he frolics after coming home all
pissed from the pub and smashes me jokingly on the mouth /
whose vomit will I clean up from the pillow as he heaves up
all over my face on Friday nights after his binge. Whose
black uniform will I press in readiness for his marches down
Brixton with the other so noble men of England / whose
photos will I dust in the living room of his heroes, Hitler,
Goebbels, Enoch, Paisley and Maggot not forgetting our
dear royals. Is it worth it any more? / I married a good
Englishman / where will I find another like that? See what
you did / and all over a stupid cheesecake.

EDDY: Wars, my dear, have been fought over less than that.

WAITRESS: I'll never find another like him.

EDDY: Yes you will.

WAITRESS: Where?

EDDY: Look no further mam than this / your spirits won me / cast
thy gaze to me / my face / and let thine eyes crawl slowly
down / that's not a kosher salami I'm carrying / I'm just
pleased to see you / sure I can do like him / polish my
knuckleduster / clean my pants / I'll give you a kicking with
the best if that's what you really want / you'll have my set of
proud photos to dust / I'd rather treat you fair and square
and touch your hair at night and kiss your sleeping nose / I'll
not defile your pillow, but spread violets beneath your feet /
I'll squeeze your toes at night if they grow cold and when we

through rose gardens walk I'll blow the aphids from your
hair / I'll come straight home from work at night not idle for
a pint and all my spunk I'll keep for thee to lash you with at
night as soft and warm as summer showers / I'll leak no
precious drop in the Camden sauna for a fiver ('don't be long
dear, others waiting') but strew the silver load in thee to dart
up precious streams / I'll heave my sceptre into thee / your
thighs I'll prise apart and sink like hot stone into butter / into
an ocean of ecstasy for that's what you are to me / an ecstasy
of flesh and blood and fluted pathways softest oils and smells
never before uncapped / I'll turn you upside down and inside
out / I'll strip you bare and crawl under your skin / I'm mad
for you / you luscious brat and madam, girl and woman
turned into one / I'll take you love for what you are!

WAITRESS: You've eased my pain you sweet and lovely boy / I
thought I'd miss him desperately but now I can when
looking at you hardly remember what he looks like. You look
so familiar to me though we have never met / so strange
perhaps the true feeling love brings to your heart. The
familiar twang.

EDDY: I feel the same for you.

WAITRESS: You remind me of someone or something.

EDDY: What, ducky?

WAITRESS: Oh, nothing.

EDDY: Confess my dear the quandary that doth crease your brow
and makes the nagging thought stay in your head, the way an
Irish fart hangs in the air long after its creator wends his
weary way to Kilburn High Street.

WAITRESS: 'Tis nothing sweet but this / I had a kid, just two he
were, sweet and blue-eyed just like you / a darling, then one
day disaster struck / and don't it just / an August trip to
Southend for the day / all hot and sticky with floss and
smiling teeth / hankies and braces / start off at Tower Pier
excitement, sandwiches and loads of fizzy Tizer.

EDDY: (Aside) Strange, I love Tizer.

WAITRESS: Then two or three miles out we hit a mine that slunk
so steadily up the Thames, like some almighty turd that

won't go down no matter how often you flush the chain, so this
had stayed afloat, it showed its scarred and raddled cheek
from its long buffets round the choppy seas and just by luck as
if the fates had ordained us to meet it blew us at the moon / at
least it made a hole so large that suddenly the Thames
resembled Brighton on a broiling day with heads a-bobbing
everywhere, my Frank swam back and I clung to a bit of raft
but little Tony, for that was his fair name, ne'er did surface up
. . . I hope his end was quick.

EDDY: No chance that some local fisherman my have snatched him
from the boiling seethe.

WAITRESS: No word, no sign, not even his little corpse did show / I
stuck around all night, then as the dawn arose I saw his little
oil-soaked teddy bear, as if heaved up from deep inside the
river's guts. It lay amidst the condoms on the junk-filled
strand. I took it home and washed it.

EDDY: That's a sad tale / and I feel grieved for you my dear that woe
should strike at one who was so young and fair / and let the
others more deserving of fate's lash to get away with murder.

WAITRESS: Fate never seems to give out where it's meant but
seems to pick you out as from a hat / like bingo and if your
number's on it boy you've had it.

EDDY: That little bear you mentioned, sweet . . . may I see the
precious relic?

WAITRESS: You really want to?

EDDY: Yeah, let's have a butcher's.
  (*She goes and brings the bear in.*)
  'Tis strange but often times I dreamed of such a thing a little
  Rufus just like this / I never had one, yet seemed to miss the
  little furry cuddly thing as if my body knew the feel whereas
  my mind could not / since then I've always liked small furry
  things. Come, love, you've had your share of woe and so have I
  and if fate heaps the shit it also heaps the gold and finding you
  is like a vein I never dreamed of, so fate's been kind this time /
  I think we're fated, love don't you?

WAITRESS: I do, my precious, for once I bless the stars that this
time made me such a man / you've got the same eyes as my

Tony – green and jadey like the sea.

EDDY: Your eyes are like the sunlight in the sea that speckles on
the rocks so deep below / all blue and gold.

WAITRESS: Your face is like all Greek / and carved from ancient
marble.

EDDY: Your body feels all soft like puppies, strong as panthers.

WAITRESS: Let's go to bed my sweet.

EDDY: OK.

DAD: Do you think that it could happen
that the curse could come about
that Ed could kill his own dad,
pop into his mother's pants, I had to kick him out.

MUM: That's something we will never know dear
until the day, when suddenly you'll
see quite a different Ed than the one that's known to me.

DAD: You're right, dead right . . . oh Dinah
what did we do that such a curse
should be blasted on the heads of me and you.

MUM: Who knows my dear what evil lies in store
that we are unaware of, did we cause some
grief somewhere, inflict some unhealed sore.

DAD: I've done nothing all my life
I've been an honest Joe
shit on that fortune teller
and his vile and evil joke.

MUM: It's funny that twice we heard it Ted
it's funny that a second time
another face years later should
sound the same old horrid warning line.

DAD: Perhaps we should have told him Dinah
perhaps we ought to tell
our son should know the secret
or we may end up in . . .

MUM: Hell you mean, you make me laugh
it's over now, it's past,
it can't be now undone with words
fate makes us play the roles we're cast.

ACT TWO

EDDY: Ten years have come and gone, scattered their leaves on us / drenched us in blazing sun and rain / toughened my sinews to combat the world. I improved the lot of our fair café by my intense efforts, aided of course by my sweet mate / got rid of sloth and stale achievement / which once was thought as normal / I made the city golden era time / the dopes just died away when faced with real octane high-power juice / the con men that have tricked you all the while with substitute and fishy watery soup / went out of business and people starved for nourishment brain-food and guts just flocked to us / the fat-faced bastards you saw sitting on expense accounts and piles / too long defied the needs of our gnawing biting hunger / real food and drink / real substance for the soul / not those decayed and spineless wonders who filled the land / strutting and farting pithy anecdotes at boring dinner parties on profits made by con and cheap / they thought they were the cream and not the sour yuk they really were / we showed them the way / they died in trying to keep up with us / they faded in a heap.

WIFE: Ten years have flown away as Apollo's Chariot hath with fiery stride lit up our summers, thawed our frosts and kissed our cheeks / ten winters hath the hoary bearded god of ice encased our earth in pinch hard grip of chill / to be kicked out in turn by spring's swift feet of Ceres, Pluto, Dionysus / and April brooks do glisten giggling over rocks and reeds so pleased to be set free / ten years this splendid symphony of life hath played its varied song / hath saddened and elated / hath drawn the sap of life into the fiery poppy and frangipani and gripped them in its autumn sleep again / whilst we my man that is and me, for three thousand three hundred and

sixty-five times did celebrate our own ritual in nights of
swooning.

EDDY: While I each day and year have scored another niche into
this world of ours / have moved about and jostled / cut a throat
or two metaphoric of course and shown how what this world
doth crave is power, class and form with a dab of genius now
and then. We cured the plague by giving inspiration to our
plates / came rich by giving more and taking less / the old-style
portion control practised by fat thieves went out with us / we
put the meat back into the sausage mate / now once more the
world will taste good / no more the sawdust and preservative
colouring and cat shit that you could better use to fill your
walls than line your stomachs / so foul that nations overseas
would ban them from their fair stalls and shops lest their
strong youth should fall into the listless British trance so often
seen in Oxford Street or on the Piccadilly Line at 8 a.m. / a
nation half asleep and drugged with foul and bestial things
poured out of packets / massed up by operators who conspired
with commies thick in plot to weaken our defences / feed the
nation shit and mother's crud and watch them crumble down
in heaps upon the pavement / then the cunning reds just blow
them over skittle-like / but now in our great chain we energize
the people, give soul food and blistering blast of protein
smack / sandwiches the size of fists chock full of juicy smile-
filled chunks / the nation blinks and staggers back to work on
this / not fast / it takes a while to use those muscles starved so
long / limp with only holding *Daily Mirror* race results / and
eyes so dim from weekly charting of the pools / we'll get them
back to work, no fear though they may die of shock upon the
way / we'll drag them out of pubs, their fingers still gripping
on the bar they know so well, like babies reluctant to part with
mother's tit / it's us that has to do it / rid the world of
half-assed bastards clinging to their dark domain and keeping
talent out by filling the entrances with their swollen carcasses
and sagging mediocrity / let's blow them all sky high, or let us
see them simply waste away as the millions come to us.
(*Chorus sing 'Jerusalem'.*)

The SPHINX.

WIFE: The plague is not quite over yet. There's still a plague
around this city darling that will not go away, caused by
some say some evil deed that has not purged itself, but
continues to rot away inside the wholesome body of our
state / people are dropping like flies / armed killers snipe
from the shattered eyes of buildings and death stalks in the
foul and pestilent breath of friends whose eyes are drunk
with envy and greed at your success / people shake your hand
with limp grips as if afraid to catch it. The illness of inertia,
and should I shan't I, the country's awash in chemicals that
soup the brain to dullness to dull the dullness of grinding
hips long bored with ancient habit and lovers are afraid to
stroke each other's groins lest new laws against spreading the
plague outlaw them. Masturbating shops line every High
Street and the pneumatic drill of strong right wrists ensures a
girl a fat living, the country's awash in spunk not threshing
and sweetening the wombs of lovers but crushed in Kleenex
and dead in cubicles with red lights. Meanwhile men in
white masks are penetrating the holy crucible where life may
have slipped in, and armed with scalpels and suction pumps
tear out the living fruit and sluice it down the river of
sewage, the future Einsteins, Michelangelos and future
Eddys. The blood and plasma of creation is swept and
flushed away with gasps of 'don't' inside the tender packages
not yet fulfilled.

EDDY: That's the plague at work all right, there's something
rotten in the city that will not die / a sphinx I read stands
outside the city walls tormenting all that pass they say and
killing those who cannot answer her strange riddle / no doubt
she helps to spread the canker and the rot and yet no one can
destroy her.

WIFE: I heard that too, and yet she can at will dissolve herself to
air.

EDDY: I'll go and sort her out.

WIFE: Be careful darling / you are all I have.

EDDY: Don't fret, if I've come this far, survived the worst that

fate can throw I'll come through this as well don't wait up I
may be late but if I'm not back by dawn, I'll meet you in
heaven, if not we'll met in hell.

SCENE 2

SPHINX *outside the walls*.

SPHINX: Who are you, little man / pip squeak scum / drip off the
prick / mistake in the middle of the night / you've come to
answer my riddle / the riddle of the sphinx / fuck off you
maggot before I tear your head off / rip your eyes out of your
head and roast your tongue / you nothing, you man / you
insult of nature go now before I lose my cool.

EDDY: I'm not afraid of you . . . you old slag / you don't scare
Eddy 'cause Eddy don't scare easy / I've beaten better than
you in Singapore brothels / you can only frighten weak men
not me / why do you exist to kill men you heap of filth / you
detestable disease / because you can't love / loveless you can
only terrify man no one could love you / who could even kiss
that mouth of yours when your very breath stinks like a
Hong Kong whorehouse when the fleet's in.

SPHINX: You make me laugh you fool man / you should know
about brothels, they exist for you to prop up your last fading
shreds / men need killing off before they kill off the world /
louse, you pollute the earth / every footstep you take rots
what's underneath / you turn the seas to dead lakes and the
crops are dying from the plague that is man / you are the
plague / where are you looking when you should be looking
at the ghastly vision in the mirror / the plague is inside you.
You make your weapons to give you the strength that you
lack / you enslave whip beat and oppress use your guns,
chains, bombs, jets, napalm, you are so alone and pathetic,
love from you means enslavement, giving means taking, love
is fucking, helping is exploiting, you need your mothers you
mother fucker, to love is to enslave a woman to turn her into
a bearing cow to produce cannon fodder to go on killing / can

you ever stop your plague / you're pathetic, unfinished, not like me, never like us, a woman, a sphinx. Women are all sphinx. I have taken the power for all, I am the power / I could eat you alive and blow you out in bubbles / I devour stuff like you . . . oh send me strong men you scrawny nothing / look what they send me / mock up heroes / plastic movie watchers / idolizer of a thousand westerns / punk hero / flaccid man / macho pig / rapist filth and shit / oh nature's mistake in the ghastly dawn of time / when women were women, androgynous and whole and could reproduce themselves but somewhere and some time a reptile left our bodies, it crawled away and became man, but it stole our little bag of seed and even since the little reptile has been trying to crawl back, but we don't want it anymore, all we need is your foul little seed, you gnat . . . something that takes you thirty seconds of your life and us nine months we create build nourish care for, grow bigger and fat and after we suckle and provide. While you dig in the earth for treasure, play your stupid male games / go you biped of dirt / just a prick followed by a heap of filth, I feel sorry for you / I really feel for you / I've eaten enough men this week / so go / fuck off / stink scum dirt shit / go, before I tear you to pieces / go and plot and scheme, hurt, exploit and rape, oppress and wound, make a few more evil laws you shrivel of flesh, you poor unreliable penis. You have not even our capacity for passion . . . I could come ten times to your one / wanna try big boy? You are from my rib mister / me from you? what a joke / woman was Adam / she was the earth, woman is the tide / woman is in the movement of the universe / our bodies obey the phases of the moon . . . our breasts swell and heave and our rich blood surges forth to tell us we are part of the movement of nature / what signs do you have? / How do you know that you are even alive? / Do you bleed / do you feel the kicking in your womb / does a mouth draw milk from your soft breast / can you tell the future / can you do anything? What signs do you have / a date with death / the hour you must attack / unable to create you must

destroy / I am the earth / I am the movement of the universe /
I am liquid, fire and all elements / my voice rises octaves high
and communicates with the spirits of the dead / my skin is
soft and velvet and desirable to those with rough faces and
bodies hard and muscled to labour, to toil across the face of
the earth for us / the goodness of life / woman / we / sex /
sphinx, the grand and majestic cunt, the great mouth of life /
the dream of men in their aching lonely nights / the eternal
joy that men die for and envy and emulate / what they sicken
for and crave for and go insane for / so go, you are small,
insignificant, piss off you worm or I'll break your teeth and
pull out your fingers / go fuck yourself or stick a bomb up
your fucking asshole you heap of murdering bastard shit filth
. . . go, you make me vomit.

EDDY: Without me you are nothing / without me you wouldn't
exist without me you are an empty screaming hole.

SPHINX: You what! You think I need you. I need milk but do I go
to bed with a cow. I'll farm and fertilize you and keep you in
pens where you will do no harm / now go boy, I am getting
aroused, be grateful that for some reason I feel for your
pathetic attempts at heroism.

EDDY: I want to answer your riddle.

SPHINX: Then you must know that those that can't answer it die,
and then if you can't I will kill you, I will tear your cock off
with my teeth before I eat you up.

EDDY: With pleasure / if I answer it / what do I gain?

SPHINX: You can kill me.

EDDY: Then I will cut off your head for women talk too much.

SPHINX: I agree. You're a brave little fart. So here goes: what
walks on four legs in the morning, two legs in the afternoon
and three legs in the evening?

EDDY: Man! In the morning of his life he is on all fours, in the
afternoon when he is young he is on two legs and in the
evenings when he is erect for his women he sprouts the third
leg.

SPHINX: You bastard, you've used trickery to find out the riddle.

EDDY: No, just reason. All right, sorry to have to do this, I was growing quite fond of you.

SPHINX: I don't care any more / to tell the truth I was getting bored with scaring everyone to death and being a sphinx / OK cut it off and get it over with.
(*He cuts off her head.*)

EDDY: She would put you off women for life / but not me / I love a woman / I love her / I just love and love and love her / and even that one / I could have loved her / I love everything that they possess / I love all their parts / I love every part that moves / I love their hair and their neck / I love the way they walk across the kitchen to put the kettle on / in that lazy familiar way / I love them when they open their eyes in the morning / I love their baby-soft skin / I love their voices / I love their smaller hands than mine / I love lying on them and them on me / I love their soft breasts / I love their eyelashes and their noses / their teeth and their shoulders / and their giggles / and their desperate passions and their liquids and their breath against yours in the night / and their snores / and their legs across yours and their feet in the morning and I love their bellies and thighs and the way each part fits into mine / and love the way my part fits into them / and love her sockets and joints and ball bearings / and love her hip bone and her love-soaked parts that want me / I love her seasons and love her sleeping and love her walking and speaking and whispering and loving and singing and love her back and her bum nestled into you and you become an armchair / and love her for taking me in / and giving me a home for my searing agonies / my lusts / my love / my dreams / my sweetness / my honey / my peace of mind / and love pouring all my love into her with open eyes and love our fatigue and love her knees and shoulder blades and pimples and love her waiting for me and love her soothing me as I tell her about my day's battles in the world – and love and love and love her and her and!

(WIFE *enters*.)

WIFE: Well done my sweet, now all will be well / my hero . . . yes
you are / my brave and shining knight / my lion, yes! And
I'm your mate / my brave and gentle lion / and now to
celebrate let's have your dear old pa and ma to dine and
reconcile the fairy tales and woes of past and be all gooey nice
together in family bliss.

EDDY: I have to laugh when I think of my soppy mum and dad /
locked up in council bliss / and £40 a week driving a 38 from
Putney down to Waltham Cross and getting clobbered each
Saturday night.

WIFE: Invite them over Ed, to share just once our colour TV,
hi-fi, home movies showing us in fair Ibiza and Thebes, of
you diving in the bright blue cobalt sea, your smiling new-
capped teeth all sparkling in the brilliant sun, invite them to
partake of our deep leather sofas / succulent wines / show our
video that records those programmes that you wish to view
when after working late at night in selfless graft you sit with
dog and slipper by your feet . . . let them enjoy the comfort
of central-heated bathroom . . . no more the cold ass on a
plastic seat but wool-covered and pipes all steaming hot, of
stairs thick-gloved in pile so soft that each tread is like a
luscious meadow. Would they not like a Slumberdown or
even our soft waterbed which thrusts our pelvises so sweetly
swished together, needlepoint shower show your mum the
joys of kitchen instant disposal waste, no washing up, just
time to enjoy our super apple pie.

EDDY: I'll send the chauffeur down to pick them up / that's if my
dad has rid himself of that old hoary myth that like a louse
ate inside his nut, to tell him of patricide and horrid incest /
or subtitled could be called the story of a mother fucker / a
tale of kiddiwinks to send them mad to bed and cringe at
shadows in the night, and in their later years to bung good
gelt to shrinks in Harley Street.

WIFE: When you told me that story Ed / I could not believe that
grown ups still could set such store by greasy gypsies in a
booth / and to kick you out all young and pink into the

seething world while you were wet behind the lugs / maybe 'twas a ruse to get you out the nest.

EDDY: Who knows my dear the wily minds of cruddy mums and dads whose heads chock full of TV swill, the pools and read your own horoscope / who believe in anything they read that comes so fluent forth from out the gushy asses of the turds in Fleeting Street / so what, it put me on the springboard young and lively and I learned how to jackknife into the surging tide with all the best.

WIFE: You're tuf that's what my love / you're a survivor in the swilling mass of teeth and knives and desperate eyes all anxious to carve out their pound of flesh / you did it and you're still a beaut / still lovely brown and svelte / success has not paunched you or stuck a fast ass on your hips or burnt an ulcer in your gut / or made your mouth a stinking ashtray where fat cigars hang like a turd that cannot be expelled / but hangs on till the end / your sweet and honey breath / your tongue's not coated with the slime of ten-course meals taken with other con artists who flash their gaudy rings and thick as pigshit wives who sit at home and wank or play some bridge with other dozy bags whose only exercise is stretching out an arm to screech out 'taxi' outside Harrods / you're sweet and your body's like a river, flowing, flowing, flowing into me / it moves like a flowing river . . . your streaming muscles carry me along your river, along your soft and hard and flowing river / when I'm in your arms I'm carried along this endless stream and then I reach the sea, I'm swept up by your sea, I'm carried by a wave, I'm threshed up in your wave and then set down again only to be re-gathered up as your volcanic wave gathers me as a piece of ocean, as your sweet lustful pangs gather up its morsel I'm swept up, I'm gathered up, I'm sucked up and spun along a raging storming river . . . I love your body, I love your fingers and round and round and tearing and gripping and finding and searching and twisting and gathering me for your sweet lustful pangs . . . and then and then and then . . . your body is like a tree . . . like branches twisting and breaking . . . like a wave like a wind,

like an animal like a lion . . . ferocious and sweet lustful
pangs grow bigger darling . . . as they grow bigger to make
your sweet spunk flow . . . they grow bigger and the lion's
breath is hot and the grip on me is growing tight and more
ferocious and then and then I know . . . that you tremble,
you shake, you quiver, you thrash . . . oh the river flows, oh
. . . it flows, oh it floods through me . . . as you tremble your
quiver is shot into me . . . oh I am flowing with the river in
the wet and warm and succulent flow . . . you turn me into a
flow and flood me . . . and the shivering and the quivering
and the shaking and the trembling, softly softly . . . softly
goes as the storm passes slowly . . . goes . . . slowly . . .
rumbling into the distance . . . slowly goes the breath less
hot, but soft and silky and sweat on your back and silky on
your thighs and warm between our thighs . . . oh / life my
love / oh love my precious / oh sweet my honey / oh heaven
my angel / oh darling my husband.

EDDY: But soft my darling wife / what noise is that / it must be my
cruddy mum and dad / who interrupt your lovely flow of gob
rich thick and pearly verbs that send my blood a-racing to
my groin so I might manufacture love-wet tides.

SCENE 4

MUM *and* DAD *enter.*

DAD: Look how he's got on / you really got on well son / I'm
proud of ya. He's got class and qualities drawn from me.

MUM: From me more, his mum whom he did love not this wet
fart that calls himself his dad.

DAD: Don't talk like that in front of Eddy's wife you sloppy-
titted, slack-assed lump, you raving scrawny dried-up witch.

MUM: Don't talk to me about my body / age has withered my soft
beauty but you will need cremating since your poisoned flesh
would cause pollution in the earth and make widespread crop
failures / you're death on two varicosed legs and a hernia
belt.

DAD: I've got no words for you Dot . . . since you were gang-
banged by that bunch of drunken darkies . . . a dozen it
were, if I counted right, whose swollen truncheons flashed
their golden sprints of foam into the sulphurous and heavy
night, since that bad time you've not been right in ye old
bonce . . . I know that night was dark for you in double
horror and I fear that it may be the cause of your unseeemly
evil tongue that like a poisoned snake doth linger under filthy
damp and rotting stone.

EDDY: Hallo dad, hallo mum – good to see ya again . . .

MUM: Oh Ed, it looks really lovely, and this is your lovely wife /
oh! how lovely, oh, she's nice.

WIFE: Why thank you, I think you're very charming yourself.

MUM: Oh thank you. You are nice, have a nice day, you're
welcome.

WIFE: Please feel free, make yourself at home, how very nice to
meet you. Have you had a good journey? How is everyone at
home? Isn't the weather cold now? It will soon be winter.
You're looking so young. You really look well. You've lost
weight. Are you going away this summer? Do you use
Fablon in your kitchen?

MUM: You've a lovely home, it's really lovely, just lovely. Some
people are lucky, some people have all the fun. Some
mothers do have 'em. Mind you, I mean, it goes to show,
well it does. Idle hands make wicked thoughts. He's all
right, really, underneath . . . when you get to know him, he's
lovely, have you been away this year? Water off a duck's
back, dear.

EDDY: So what's the news my folks / my flesh and blood / chip off
the old / apple of your / say what goes on in my old
neighbourhood / where once rank violence stalked the dirty
streets and filthy yobbos hung round the corners of old pubs
like flies on dead carrion / say can you still walk down the
streets at night? Or do you macaroni in your pants at every
shadow that stalks out lest it be some Macdougal out to line
his coat with other's hard-earned gelt . . . around this manor
there's peace my folks. Move out that council flat where

urchins' piss does spray the lift which takes you to your eyrie on the twenty-fifth floor and move in with us, or do you still fear that old curse / that bunch of gypsy bollocks, that you so avidly did gulp / though secretly me thinks you used that as a ruse, to clear me out the womb and save yourself some L.s.d. / you always said I'd eat you out of house and home / round here only the poodles drop their well-turned turds in little piles so neat. And au pair girls go pushing little Jeremys into the green and flowery parks / no ice-cream vans come screaming round this manor / all's quiet / just the swish on the emerald lawns close cropped like the shaven heads of astronauts / and in the quiet of the evening silly chit chat from the strangled vocal cords of well-heeled neighbours rises from the gardens as they wolf down in the summer nights a half a dozen gin and tonics. Nicely tired from a hard day's graft of thieving in the city. So come and stay. You're welcome and bring the cat as well, we've always got room for moggie.

DAD: Nah son but thanks and double ta. You're very kind to us . . . how thoughtful / bless you, you're welcome, have a nice day, but we're used to wot we got, can you teach an old dog new tricks, a bit long in the tooth you're as old as you feel, and I feel like a worn out old fart . . . we know the familiar faces / our rotten neighbours / the geezer who collects the payments on the fridge and on the telly every week / meals on wheels that daily calls now that we're getting older, all familiar trappings that have trapped us / now that our useful working life has been sucked dry by the state we get a little pension and some security for which I sign / now that my boss god bless him sits back fat and greasy / not that I mind, he got it by hard graft and cunning / good luck to him / he gave me fifty quid when I retired, handsome and a watch with fifteen jewels / right proud I was / so what I got asbestos in my lung / so what I got coal dust in my blood / so what I got lead poisoning in my brain / so what I got shot nerves from the machines / so what I lost two fingers in the press / so what I'm going deaf from the steel mills / so what I lost a lung

for our old king in Dunkirk / I'd do it again / yes I would I
tell ya / so what I got fuck all for it from our fair state / so
what they're gliding past in their Rolls-Royces / and their fat
little kids come tumbling out on piggy little legs / so what
they thieve and murder and get away with it / so what our
lovely royals pay no tax / they're figureheads mate / so what I
starve waiting for your cheque which sometimes you forget
to send if you are busy entertaining, when you forget your
old ma and pa . . . son!

MUM: Don't listen Ed, he's gone a bit in the nut since they retired
him / all he does is grouse and quail. When you complain
remember others worse off than you / I think of mothers
whose sweet fruit of their most holy wombs / those warm and
precious sacks of giggling joy, who have been snatched by
sex-mad fiends. They stalk around the town . . . there are so
many around / you cannot pick up the daily snot-picker these
days without seeing between the tits and race results the
photos of the burns and scalds and broken limbs . . . the
staring eyes of kids / how one is burnt by fag ends / others
punched black and blue / screams in the night / neighbours
too scared or fastened to *Hawaii Five-O* to receive the
bloated cries that stab through the walls like an open hand
saying help me / others, babies with broken lips, their little
ribs all smashed by dads who have caught the British plague
that cements their heads and puts vitriol inside their hearts /
some kids chained to their beds for hours at a time and others
crawling in shit and piss . . . and whack and zunk goes mum
and splatter back hand crack goes dad . . . one kid's nipples
almost burnt off . . . what about the dad who picked up his
small innocent and smashed his head against the wall, until
his brains seeped out . . . what dreams did that kid have as
his grey thoughts ran down the wallpaper . . . and then the
judge says . . . 'off you go, you are basically a good character'
. . . and then he's off to celebrate in the nasty pub with his
old lady . . . and up and down the length and breadth the
straps are out and babies, bairns and kids are straightened
out, lashed out, whipped and made to obey, the nation's full

of perverts if you ask me / the plague still flourishes mate.

EDDY: The plague mum / the plague is still about? You never did nuffin like that to me / you only gave me muffins and jam / swaddles of lovey love and spoiling and playing and story-telling. And swishing my pillow and a ride on dad's back and chase around the garden, and a three-wheel bike. You only gave me ten slices of toast every morning and Marmite after school . . . I looked all Bisto like, and like those kids whose shoes have a long way to go I was put on a path called bliss with jammy mouth and sticky doughnut fingers / a dad who put me on the crossbar of his bike and never once introduced the back of his hand to my bonce not once opened his eyes wide and hate-filled and sought to venge some filthy taste for colouring my flesh in Chartreuse green or bruisy blue. No! We'd race across the municipal lido. How long can you stay under. *Dandy* and the *Beano* each week and even the *Film Fun* as well.

DAD: You were loved son / we wanted to give you love / we luved ya kid. You know . . . like open hands gripping your shoulders and a squeeze at the end . . . palm on your head and ruffling your hair, a clenched fist and a slow tap on the chin . . . like chin-up when you didn't pass your eleven-plus 'cause you were a dummy . . . I didn't want you to hate us.

EDDY: Hate? I never used that word my folks, only pocket money each week five bob and Sat morn flicks. Do you mean to say you loved me because you were afraid I'd hate you? 'Cause the gypsy's curse rang in your ears? Let's smother him with spoiling and cuddling so he won't want to hurt his old dad, you make me laugh . . . you would have loved me the same without the rotten curse / I'm your flesh and blood, it's natural.

DAD *and* MUM: But you're not our son, son.

EDDY: SHIT GIVE UP THE GEN / SPILL YOUR GUTS / OPEN YOUR NORTH AND SOUTH AND LET ROLL THE TURDS BEFORE I PONEY MY Y-FRONTS. IN OTHER VERBS OPEN YOUR CAKE-HOLE AND UTTER. LET ME EARWIG YOUR

HOBSONS. NOT YOUR SON. OH BOLLOCKS AND CRACKLOCK.

WIFE: Don't say that he ain't your real produce of your blood-swept thighs, not shoved out of your guts in warm sticky afterbirth, not the sparkle in his dad's eye in the glinting night when his pa heaved apart his woman's limbs and unloaded a binful of hot spunk, not eyed her like a lodestone or a star, or a jewel in the corner of his eye not breathed hard or pulse raced to produce this lovely hunk of super delicious wondrous beefy darling spunky guy / not seen you walking from behind and wanted to grasp your arse and deliver the mail up your wet and wondrous letterbox?

MUM: Nah! 'Fraid not!

WIFE: Oh fuck.

EDDY: So what if I'm adopted / who gives a monkey's tit.

DAD: Like this it was. Crics and groans, shouts and shrieks. I was fishing by Wapping, just down from the *Prospect of Whitby* . . . a peaceful Sunday (you were fished out, what a find, what I prayed for, a son) threw my line, the big steamers going out to Southend. The old Tower Bridge opening up to allow the steamers' funnels through like some big lazy East End tart from Cable Street opening her thighs . . . on the deck in the sun the people of Bow, Whitechapel and Islington in their cheese-cutters and chokers, all doing a bit of a dance on the deck, the streamers flickering, the Guinness pouring . . . us waving from the shore as the old steamer cuts through the scummy old Thames and sends the swell over to us and makes our little boats kneel and bob as she passes by. When all of a sudden boy / the sun's up high, Hitler's just topped hisself. It's hot. Churchill's in command, there's peace at last. Twenty million dead / including my two boys, the radio plays we'll meet again and mares eat oats and does eat oats and little lambs eat ivy, remember. Well all of a sudden in that hot August afternoon no bananas in the shops and coupons for four ounces of sweets each week, pictures of Auschwitz just come out / thousands of bodies like spaghetti all entwined / all done in

the name of Adolf / all of a sudden in the hot blue day . . .
they're all swimming look at them, look at all that blood and
oil, bad mix, the sky turned black. What a terrific hell of a
bang, and soot is dropping all over us plus bits of people, all
the fish dropped dead, from shock, hey let's shalp them out.
Look let's get some help, they're all in the water. Some jerry
ball of hate stacked full of painful promise and carrying the
names of the future dead blew the Southend tripper to the
moon and down they fell in a deadly mash of Guinness and
Gold Flake . . . come on mate . . . 'I'll give you a hand'. We
pulled them in all night, the others just bloated up like
funfair freaks. Come on mum, don't fret, 'ere have a cuppa,
where's your little Johnnie? . . . now, now he'll be all right,
can he swim? No . . . oh. We'll find him . . . won't we lads
. . . we'll find the little bleeder . . . shine your torch over here
Bert, yeah, there's an old lady, give us your hand love, I'll
pull you in . . . oh no, just a stump, she left it in the water
. . . what bastard could do this . . . more blankets . . . bring
more tea . . . there's just not enough of us . . . there's not
enough people to help, who does this to people! What sick
perverted bastard started all this shit . . . if he was in front of
me, I would take a butcher's fucking knife and carve him
slowly bit by fucking dirty piece and feed it to the river rats
and any cunt that supports him, I'd fucking throw them in
acid baths . . . when all had gone and the dawn arose we saw
what seemed a little doll clinging to a piece of wood but on
closer butchering revealed a little bugger of about two he
were, struggling like the fuck and gripping in his paw a
greasy old big bear, which no doubt helped to keep him up.
We threw the bear back in the slick, and lifted the toddler
out all dripping wet and covered in oil looking like a darkie
so, no one about we took him home and washed him / he was
a beaut / and mum was double chuffed to see a little round
soft ball of warm goo goo / 'don't want to give him up' quoth
Dinah, 'must we' she said. 'Nah', I said 'his mum will think
he'd dead anyway' / so let her go on thinking it / but think
our Dinah rightly slurps of how its real mum will fret and

pine and waste away and mourn for her sweet lovely soft
flesh of her own / 'all right' I says 'we'll keep him for one day
only and then give him back.' A day turned into two / then
after a week we thought the shock now would be too great
and that the true mum would be adjusted to her sad loss.

WIFE: Oh shit and piss and fuck. I just pissed in my pants. (*She
faints.*)

EDDY: My dearest wife and now my mum, it seems, this lady was
the very one whose baby you snatched / she told me the
selfsame and bitter tale of how she lost her Tony and if you
found him then I am he, he whom you found that belonged
to her was me. The he you stole and gave to her did once
belong to she . . . nice to see ya, have a nice day, so I am the
squelchy mass of flesh that issued from out the loins of my
dear wife / oh rats of shit / you opened a right box there
didn't you, you picked up a stone that was best left with all
those runny black and horrid things intact and not nibbling
in my brain. So the man I verballed to death was my real
pop / the man to whom my words like hard-edged shrapnel
razed his brain / was the source of me, oh stink / warlock and
eyes break shatter, cracker and splatter . . .! / Who laughs?
Me who wants to clean up the city / stop the plague destroy
the sphinx / me was the source of all the stink / the man of
principle is a mother fucker / oh no more will I taste the
sweetness of my dear wife's pillow . . . no more . . . no more
. . . so I left my cosy and love-filled niche now so full of
horror / foul incest and babies on the way which if they come
will no doubt turn into six-fingered horrors with two heads /
poor Eddy. Oh this madness twisting my brain / I walked
through the plague rot streets and witnessed the old and the
broken / the funny faces staring out of the dead vinyl flats /
the flickering shadows of the TV tube / I sat in cafés and
thought of my desirable lovely succulent and honey-filled
wife and as I sat and stared at the rheumy faces and the dead
souls with their real wives who were plastered forever in casts
of drab compromise, my own wife seemed like a princess / I
fastened her face on the horizon like the rising moon and

stared forever into space / and when the café closed I sat and
stared forever and forever, ran through in my mind every
combination of her face and smile and eyes and twists and
curves of her lips, I sat and projected her picture on the
moon and pored through every page of our life together like a
great holy bible of magic events I examined every feature of
her landscape and ate up every part of her and loved every
part whose sum total made up this creature, my wife. And
then the moon turned as red as blood / the clouds raced
across her face and became her hair and then her eyes and the
wind pulled her hair over her face / like it did when we
walked together through the fields and the forests, when the
trees shivered and the sun kissed us and the universe
wrapped us round in a cloak of stars and rain and crushed
grass and ice-creams and teas and clenched fingers / hold on
to me / hold on to me and I will hold on to you and I'll never
let you go, hold on to me, does it matter that you are my
mother, I'll love you even if I am your son / do we cause each
other pain, do we kill each other, do we maim and kill, do we
inflict vicious wounds on each other? We only love so it
doesn't matter mother, mother it doesn't matter. Why
should I tear my eyes out Greek style, why should you hang
yourself / have you seen a child from a mother and son / no.
Have I? No. Then how do we know that it's bad / should I be
so mortified? Who me. With my nails and fingers plunge in
and scoop out those warm and tender balls of jelly quivering
dipped in blood. Oedipus how could you have done it, never
to see your wife's golden face again, never again to cast your
eyes on her and hers on your eyes. What a foul thing I have
done, I am the rotten plague, tear them out Eddy, rip them
out, scoop them out like ice-cream, just push the thumb
behind the orb and push, pull them out and stretch them to
the end of the strings and then snap! Darkness falls. Bollocks
to all that. I'd rather run all the way back and pull back the
sheets, witness my golden-bodied wife and climb into her
sanctuary, climb all the way in right up to my head and hide
away there and be safe and comforted. Yeh I wanna climb

back inside my mum. What's wrong with that? It's better than shoving a stick of dynamite up someone's ass and getting a medal for it. So I run back. I run and run and pulse hard and feet pound, it's love I feel it's love, what matter what form it takes, it's love I feel for your breast, for your nipple twice sucked / for your belly twice known / for your hands twice caressed / for your breath twice smelt, for your thighs, for your cunt twice known, once head first once cock first, loving cunt holy mother wife / loving source of your being / exit from paradise / entrance to heaven.

(*Blackout.*)

SINK THE BELGRANO!

CHARACTERS

MAGGOT SCRATCHER
PIMP
NIT
CHORUS
COMMAND
TELL
WOODY
TOMMY
PRESIDENT OF ARGENTINA
FEET
SIR FISH FACE
REASON
SAILORS
FARMERS

For Clara

Sink the Belgrano! was first performed at the Half Moon Theatre
on 2 September 1986. The cast was as follows:

MAGGOT SCRATCHER	Maggie Steed
PIMP	Barry Stanton
NIT	Bill Stewart
CHORUS	Rory Edwards
COMMAND	Terence McGinty

Other parts were played by Tom Dean Burn, George Dillon,
Eugene Lipinski and Edward Tudor Pole.

Director	Steven Berkoff
Designer	Ellen Cairns
Music	Mark Glentworth

This production of *Sink the Belgrano!* subsequently transferred to
the Mermaid Theatre, when MAGGOT SCRATCHER was played by
Louise Gold.

THE SET

The stage was divided into three areas. Upstage, on a rostrum
running left and right, was the political area with desk, and
behind it a large screen for projecting images. Downstage, on the
main playing area, was drawn the outline of a huge submarine.
The actors playing chorus and submarines would do their 'work-
outs' and acting from this area. Stage left was a pub area which
represented the 'voice of England'. Here the sailors would recline
as the people back home and relate to the news as it came in.
There was just a round table in the pub area and a dartboard
facing off stage. Music accompanied the action, marked entrances
and exits, and created a very strong atmosphere under the deft
handling of Mark Glentworth. The actors played all the roles
from Falkland farmers to Members of Parliament and, of course,
the main roles as young, physically fit submariners. Props were
kept to a minimum and were largely a change of hat or a red and

white football scarf. The sailors wore track suits throughout which was a simple neutral uniform. The chorus were dressed in plain suits. I have not indicated the kind of slides I used since this would be a personal choice, but I have indicated where it might be necessary to project the text on to the screen.

S.B.

THE STILL SMALL VOICE OF TRUTH

CHRONICLE OF INCONSISTENCIES

On Tuesday 4 May, 1982, the House of Commons heard a statement from the then Secretary of State for Defence, John Nott. People, Press and Parliament were given to understand that the forty-four-year-old USS *Phoenix*, survivor of Pearl Harbor, for such the *Belgrano* was, had to be sunk by our nuclear submarine, because she was converging on the Task Force. Albeit there had until that moment been no British casualties in action, I and others did not criticize. Daily from 2 April, we had publicly opposed the sending of the Task Force, and urged its return, but we recognized that terrible things happen, once conflict starts. No *Belgrano* – No *Sheffield*, No *Ardent*, No *Antelope*, No *Atlantic Conveyor*, No *Coventry*, No Bluff Cove, No Goose Green. But Mrs Thatcher would have been deprived of the Military Victory, which was what, for her, the Falklands War was all about.

I began to ask questions about the *Belgrano* in July 1982, when HMS *Conqueror* returned to the West Coast of Scotland. The Captain, Commander Christopher Wreford-Brown, DSO, made it clear that he had sunk the *Belgrano*, not on the impulse of defending the Task Force, but 'on orders from Northwood'. This was very different from the impression given to Parliament, Press, and People. Small inconsistencies tend to be part of larger inconsistencies – small lies part of larger lies. For example, it was dragged out of Ministers that *Belgrano* had been detected not on 2 May at 8 p.m., but on 30 April at 4 p.m. A series of Parliamentary Questions and Debates, the Old Bailey Trial of Clive Ponting, the Minority Report of the Foreign Affairs Select Committee published in July 1985, add up to a picture of a Prime Minister, aware of the Peruvian Peace Proposals, ordering the sinking of the *Belgrano*, at Chequers, on 2 May, not for reasons of military necessity but for reasons of political advantage.

Tam Dalyell MP, July, 1986

It had to be written. What a story! All those statements and contradictions in the House of Commons. All those 'statesmen' lying their little heads off in the Commons, and then when the facts emerged having to contradict themselves. What a pack of fakes, and what a disgusting bunch of rogues. It is apparent to everyone that the sinking of the *Belgrano* was a very dubious affair and led to the severe attacks on the British Fleet and subsequent huge loss of life. How many people realize that before that calculated piece of sabotage not one British soldier had died! After unloosing that torpedo under orders not from the submarine *Conqueror* but from England on a ship way outside the demilitarized zone all havoc broke loose. It was a calculated gamble to end the war at a stroke and failed miserably. My play deals with the situation as I found it and was inspired by the book by Arthur Gavshon and Desmond Rice. I met Desmond on New Year's Eve in 1984 and mutually expressing our disgust on the incident of the *Belgrano* sinking led him to introduce his book to me. It made a fascinating and sordid read. I could never understand people who could order the taking of life so easily and weep later at the havoc they caused. I imagine such people to be 'armoured' in the full Reichian sense, dead to all real human response except what concerns them personally. The lack of imagination to foresee events is typical of right-wing thinking. The pollution of the environment and their lame excuses for not dealing with it; the deadly poisoning of our seas with nuclear wastes; acid rain; bursting prisons – all seem to have one common heritage and that to me is an abnormal disregard for human life and values. Plus an overwhelming and religious belief in the sanctity of the marketplace. The *Belgrano* sinking was a typical product of that muddled and opportunist thinking. The irony is that brave Britons and Argentinians lost their lives needlessly. The play received mixed reviews and some virulent ones from the right-wing press. It was curious that their reviews, which were almost hysterical cant, resembled so closely the threats and poisoned mail I received from Fascist thugs. Special thanks to

Desmond Rice and a special thanks to the Half Moon Theatre, and Chris Bond, who took the chance and gave his unstinting support.

CHORUS: Oh you most brave and valiant Englishmen
Who never shall, no never bear the yoke
Of shame or curdled pride beneath the boot
Of some o'erweening greasy foreign bloke.
We smashed the damned Spanish might . . .
We put the Hun upon the British rack,
The Boers we kicked to kingdom come
And now the Argies sneaked behind our back.
Oh blasted glory for a few frail days
Oh cowards hiding under the sheep
Like Ulysses they sneaked while Britain dazed
Worn out with strikes and social strife
Numb with queues of unemployed that add
Their groaning weight to the nation's back . . .
But once aroused, oh ho! old Albion snorts
The Bulldog, start-eyed, drools for Argy blood
Outraged its precious garden overrun
By foreign, greasy, dark unholy scum.
Oh howl fair noble Grand Bretagne
Your people's voices crying out from afar
Like babies howling for the mother's breast
While dark satanic forces raid its nest
We put the greedy scavenger to flight
With fists of steel and hawk-like Harrier jets
Our submarines like silent hungry sharks
Went hunting for the juicy Argy game
But they were cautious, hiding, wouldn't show
Hoping for a *fait accompli* for their crime
And crawling behind the skirts of the UNO.

PIMP: Oh shit your royal sweetest Maggot,
The lousy Argy swines unleashed their bile
On us, decided to invade our Falkland
Paradise, and dead of night they came like rats
Disturbed the peace and placed their rot,
Which means their scummy Argy flag upon our
Holy God-gave Promised Land!

MAGGOT: Those bloody junta bloody swine . . .!
    How dare they, how simply do they bloody dare
    When we've been so damned good to them
    Never complained when their death squads
    Got rid of opposition in mass graves . . .
    Nor publicly showed our disgust at torture
    For those that disobeyed (since naturally we
    Wish to trade) and now those greasy Argy wogs
    Show their thanks by stealing our sweet
    Precious lands. Call out the Fleet, get planes
    And tanks, I love to have a crisis on my hands.
PIMP: We'll get the UNO behind us first
    Give evidence and facts to thwart their claim.
MAGGOT: What bloody claim! When gangsters rob
    What fuels their greed, you Pimp, is gain.
    Don't talk to me of robbers justifying
    Deeds, the land is ours, that's plain to see.
PIMP: I know that and you know that but they
    May say that we, that is those ghosts of past
    Who made up our great history, did steal it,
    Pardon the expression, first . . . in 1833 we staked
    Our claim, backed by a warship, ma'am, or two
    And threw the Argies off the land, and now
    Although through time it's ours . . . like some
    Adopted babe we suckled, and watched it grow
    Like our own flesh, the mother wants it back again.
    So let's go to the world's great states
    And get them behind us in our claim
    The child we reared must then decide
    The Islanders' wishes cannot be denied
    And naturally all of them will want to stay British.
MAGGOT: No! No! No! That's not the way, not that.
    To sit around, regurgitate old tales
    Who owned it then and now and chat
    Until we grow old, like ancient cronies in a pub
    Recounting how we owned this piece of sod
    Discounting claims and waving old contracts

Possession is you know nine-tenths the law
And he who transgresses our hard-won right
Will get himself one hell of a bloody fight.

PIMP: We must of course recourse to written law
'Tis true that they have stolen our sweet lands
But then there will be time the world will judge
Without perhaps a punch-up strewn in blood
To save lives surely is the way
With honour we will live another day.

MAGGOT: Oh bloody bollacks compromise you mean
And wait in turn for others to redeem our wealth
And sit in calm compliance while we hope
For others to present to us a deal,
While whispering give up old colonial ties
As they in turn make profits with their trade
Their greed to capture markets far and wide
Will sugar every bloody thing they say
And in the end we'll give the bloody lot away!
By the way Pimp . . . where is the Falklands??

Falkland Farmers

FARMER 1: Oh toil, oh strife, oh bleeding blooding graft
Is this the life for us I daily spout?
For sixty quid a week they bleed our veins
And us poor farmers slave for next to nought
We live in this pisspot, this dreary rock
Where no one has invested, not a jot . . .
The profits never go to thee or me,
Where then? The bloody bleedin' FIC.

FARMER 2: What's that?

FARMER 1: The bloody Falkland Island Company!

FARMER 2: What's that . . .?

FARMER 1: Those who pontz from distant lands
Who own more than forty per cent
Of this, this wind-spat spit of rock,
And take the wool, our precious locks,

They own our house, they keep us poor
And we buy our grub at the company store.
FARMER 2: So bloody bleedin' bloomin' hell
While we sit on this blasted heath
They chat about our future rights
And say our wishes must be paramount
Bollacks and lockjaw, scum and dregs!
They've done sweet FA all these years
No roads are built, no hospitals . . .
When we are ill or hurt we fly
To Argy land where Argy hands
Repair our broken bodies or we'd die
So all that's cock and bollacks when they say
We fight for you dear folks in case one day
The Argies make you drive the right-hand way.
FARMER 1: It makes good PR back in gutter press
Who suck up lies more quickly than
Do buzzing flies the garbage in a bin.
They leave behind their maggot worms
That crawl across their daily sheets,
You think the Government has a heart
In thinking of the welfare of us men?
When really their souls couldn't give a fart.
Oh bullshite soggy Scratcher spews
Her eyes are on some distant parts
Antarctica or oil, that makes a start . . .
PIMP: How dare you pigs complain, you dogs
You curs that *want* always and gripe
Then know we care for you like we
Might care for chickens in our pens
You've never had it quite so good
Regular employment, lots of space
And all you do is trim some wool
And drink yourselves into an early grave
Of course we can't worry for you.
Eighteen hundred poor souls that sweat
And piss their lives away in hell

More than that number's killed themselves
Died by their own hand from dire grief
Of unemployment while millions weep.
The nation's fit and young queue up
In grey drab cities where empty days
Will lead to pointless nights, 'Time please'
And at the end your dole queue pay.

MAGGOT: So you think how lucky you are here
You might be back in England's drear
And pleasant land where miners strike
And other left-wing pests unite
Like filthy dogs disturb our rest . . .
Now shuffle off and do some work
While we take on the nation's pain
You're useless, any excuse to shirk,
You're lucky to have me, so don't complain . . .

NIT: (Rushing on) Oh, your precious whitened hairs
Though now so stained with Sassoon's dyes
Would stand on end if now you knew
How Argentina plotted and spied.

MAGGOT: Stop spitting in my tea, you nit,
Inform me where and when this came
Catastrophe, who can we blame!!
The Labour Party, they failed, you tit.
Wake up, you git, we need a war . . .
Establish once again our might and strength
Shake our old mane, out fly the moths
Oh God, I start to feel myself again
Now where is this damn Falkland Isle?

NIT: 'Tis just a tiny spot of land
That sits so neat in threshing seas
Not far but far enough 'tis nearer
To the Argentines than us I fear.
Some eight thousand sea miles from Cornwall's toe
And stands four hundred miles from Argy shores
Which thus have tempted them to claim
The Malvinas are theirs once again.

MAGGOT: Again! Again! They never were, you mug.
They're British damn you sink that in your bontz.
Again! Just 'cause they leapt across the straits
While we were napping, dealing with the world
They sought to steal our gateway to the south
That precious stepping stone that we may need
Since raging conflict 'twixt the super states
May give a base to our dear USA.
Suppose the Commie swine made use of it
Oiling the Argy hand with swingeing bribe
Eh? What then? Tell me that, you silly prat.

NIT: A dame of iron, for that is what you are,
They never will question your metal now.
Bring forth men soldiers only for thy
Undaunted metal should compose nothing but wars.

CHORUS: And so the valiant British soldiered on
Girded their loins with Vulcan steel
The forge breathed fire night and day
Preparing ships stacked full of cannon shells
Like giant whales of death they steamed ahead
The Harriers like mosquito's wings
Did leap up in the sky were thirty-two
Next stomach loaded full like gorged beasts
Dread bombers, sixteen Victors tore the air
Armed to the teeth with missiled brains
To smell the Argy fear and chase
Locked on to their frightened fleeing game
Next, Scimitar and Scorpion tanks
As deadly as their name suggests,
Mine-sweepers . . . laser-guided bombs
Four hundred thousand tons of fuel
One hundred thousand tons of freight
To concentrate our Scratcher's boys
Into one deadly fist of hate.
We made a bridge across the seas
Which measured some eight thousand miles

And poured twenty-eight thousand noble men
To gain back our sweet Falkland Isles . . .

Inside the submarine *Conqueror*

TOMMY: All right we've heard the news let's get stuck in,
     And sail our deadly turd-shaped tube
     That will unleash pure havoc when
     Upon the surface of the deep we spy
     Some vessel filled with Argentines
     And shit some pain as it glides by
     With hunter-killer submarines
     Deep down we'll dive into the ocean's guts
     And wait . . . just still and silent till
     At last we see that great fat ship
     And then at last we'll have our . . .
CREW: (Sing) 'Sweet violets . . .'
SAILOR 1: Here, hang about and just a mo'
     Before we get all bleedin' hot
     Now sod all this, don't swallow shit
     Don't gulp down all you hear you fool
     You ape, you asshole that is used
     By others who make up the rules
     'You're just a soldier now, go kill'
     'Go Fido, fetch'. Don't think mate, no,
     Don't use no skill . . .
     Just obey orders that's your job
     Become a murderer's right hand . . .
     Don't dare to question what we do
     For what we are protecting and for who!
SAILOR 2: Protecting life and limb and British soil
     Sod you, who do you think made war?
     Who stepped upon the British corn?
     Who, mate, bloody started this all?
     For self-determination of the Falkland folk
     To make an omelette you gotta break some yolks.
SAILOR 1: What's self-determination mate?

Do you know what the fuck it means?
You just shove big words down your throat
Like when mum gave you medicine . . .
Now open up and down it goes, good boy.
Whenever hard truth won't go down
We grease the way with subtle quotes,
Self-determination, paramount, law and order,
All that crap. Old Adolf smashed Slovakia
To protect his German hordes
Sudetenland must have, he said,
Self-determination for those Nazi bores.

SAILOR 3: Then fuck off off this boat you cunt
Don't fucking winge, you got no guts
A soldier's life's obey the Queen
The thinking's done by Whitehall nuts
We know there's right and wrong on both
But basically we trust our state
You must believe in England's green
And pleasant or fucking emigrate.

SAILOR 1: I'll fight . . . I'll hold a gun . . . I'll kill
I'll support the Union Jack, so help me I will
But I'll not stuff a sock in it
I'll not become a sponge for all
Just use your brains and think at last
Before it's blown away because
You kept your brainbox up your ass.

COMMAND: Now, now, lads, let's cool it down, eh?
The bloody war's not our responsibility
Now is it? Bloody hell . . . just think
If we had to unscramble every wrong,
Undo the twisted knot of history each time
We sink a foreign ship with our sweet bombs
We'd spend our time in Davy Jones'
Deep down still gassing, who did wrong?
Or else blown up upon the choppy green
Discussing politics as we cling
To shattered mast heads in the freezing sea.

No, boys, you volunteered, you came aboard
Because you like the adverts on TV
You want to be a hero, fire a gun . . .
Wear fancy helmets in your jets
As you ascend into the sky like Zeus
Like a god, omnipotent, a silver bird.
With nuclear claws you tear and kill
Or else beneath the deep as deadly sharks
Your finger on the button, death all round
You deal your piercing strike and wait
Until the bomb slips silently, no sound
Is made until it swiftly penetrates
Like a hot knife into butter . . .
It sinks into the bowels of the ship
Into steel plate it cuts and rips
And from the wounds issue its life
Machines and oil, smoke and blood
And then the sea replaces all that space
And claims the ship like carrion back again
That's why you're here, yes, that's your job!

SAILOR 1: I see, we're just a bunch of yobs.
COMMAND: That's right, you've got it, boy,
Don't look for principles in politics
It's just a game they play, you're Whitehall's toys
You're here to kill or die, not reason bloody why
Did we go in 'gainst bloody Ian Smith
When he seized power in '65? . . . No Task Force
Then rushed in and said we're here to defend
Rhodesia's black men . . .
And do not think for old Hong Kong
We'll go in there and fight, no fear,
China's a bit too big for us my dear.

SAILOR 1: So it's all a question of size or race?
COMMAND: You've got it sonny in this case
You're the Task Force boys . . . we rule the waves
'Cause if you don't, you'd better pray.

Cabinet

MAGGOT: Where's my Foreign Secretary Pimp
And get me my good faithful Nit
Those two defenders of Tory strength.

PIMP and NIT: Here your worship most honoured Maggot.

MAGGOT: Well, what's the news today my boys?
Come on Pimp don't slobber and winge,
If the news is bad just spit it out
I've not all day to see you cringe
I must get Denis's supper soon,
And if you don't unheave your load
I'll not get the best sides of bacon home
So don't annoy me with your stutter
Just open your cake-hole and sodding utter.

PIMP: It's good and bad oh holy Scratcher.

MAGGOT: (Aside) *I loathe these fair and foul male turds*
Still, I'll throw them out but screw them first.

PIMP: They want to make with us peace terms.

MAGGOT: They bloody what? Why peace terms now?
After they shit on our front door.

PIMP: It seems (well not exactly our front door
More like the garden gate or tradesman's
Entrance so to speak) . . .
It seems that having made their little *coup*
Or *fait accompli* . . . it's up to you.
They're willing now to sue for peace, i.e.
A recognition of their claims . . .
Historic rights when Spain left Argentina
How Malvinas are to them their symbol
Of the time when they kicked Spain
Right up the ass and now they want
To introduce the boot to us . . .

NIT: We seized the place in 1833 and now
It's been so long it really does belong
To us . . . it's practice . . . it's ours . . .
For a century or more our folk

Have toiled the soil and reared their young.
MAGGOT: Oh shut up, Nit, you'll make me weep
And anyhow who asked you to speak
Just shut your trap, you're M.o.D.
That means defence if you can't read.
I have a well-paid politician here
Called Pimp who interprets history
Or bends it here and there if there
Be need . . . What say you, Pimp, the world's with us?
Have you checked old Cowboy yet,
Old Geriatric Joe, is he for us?
PIMP: Without a doubt, he's for us like you
Can't believe . . . sends all his love
And will give all the info that we need.
Like how much weaponry they've got and where
How many planes, what ships, what subs,
He'll loan his radar, high frequency
To intercept and translate any code
That they may send, just point your
Guns and trust him, he'll do the rest.
MAGGOT: Oh Jolly Joe . . . old Cowboy Poke
Oh what a friend indeed when times
Are tough and then a friend we need
To help us smooth the way . . .
How sweet . . . He said all that? Aah Joe
I must invite the old sod back . . .
His wife's though such an evil bore
Why is it great blokes marry such whores?
BOTH: Hmmmn . . . hmmnnnn . . . hmmmmn ?!
MAGGOT: Oh never mind . . . just fuck all that,
Oh shit . . . a pound of bacon with no fat
I'll be back, just chat away . . .
I've got to get the groceries . . .
And please don't quarrel when I've gone
Or plot behind my back!! You scum.
BOTH: My lady . . . would we do that?
PIMP: Oh fuck, oh shit, oh piss, oh balls.

NIT: What's the problem old boy . . . Do let me hear.
PIMP: We just bloody sold to Argentina
    Some missiles and some naval weaponry
    Two hundred million quids' worth flogged
    Which may be used against our Fleet
    Oh hot bollacks and spotted dick
    Our own weapons may like to find
    Their way back to their master's house
    Weapons of death carry no names
    The more's the problem, who can we blame?

SAILOR 1: Dear Tina, we've passed the Canary Isle
    One periscope-depth run each thirty hours
    Just to keep us on our toes
    This is beginning to feel like fun.

NIT: Oh Pimp, you pontz, you prat, you cur . . .
    You, the Foreign Secretary, that what you are?
    Did you not suspect that one day
    The bloody Argies would get itchy feet
    And aim their guns at the British Fleet!
PIMP: Who was to know? Well not for sure
    We sell death weapons to those who
    Pay. Who cares who they kill, it's their war,
    We only manufacture death, no more.
    We don't tell who to shoot and kill
    We flog the bloody stuff, that's all . . .
    But usually it's not our doorstep
    We have deigned to shit upon.
    South Africa's too far away . . .
    We made a bomb in Lebanon . . .
    Excuse me! . . . I mean a killing . . .
    Oh no! I mean we made a fortune
    Selling death all round the world
    Is it my fault that now by chance
    A bloody boomerang's been hurled?

SAILOR 2: Dear Janet, we've been going five days
 I miss you but it won't be long
 I'll take some pics, the blokes are nice
 For supper we had ice-cream and rice.

MAGGOT: (re-entering) Well done . . . I got the last half-
  pound . . .
 He likes it lean and meaty . . . don't we all.
 Bastards were just about to close,
 I said now what's all this, you work part-time?
 The Brits are such a lazy bunch of sods
 No wonder there's three million unemployed.
 The buggers simply now refuse to work
 And then the Labour scum will point at me
 It's not our bloody sodden fault
 It's dole money the state doles out,
 They get for free by queueing up
 Just once a week, not so much less
 Than they would get in full-time graft.
NIT: Then ma'am, why not get wages up?
 And so temptation's not so great
 The difference being far too much
 Between the dole and a week well paid!
MAGGOT: No!! . . . Get *dole* down, and then you'll see
 A scramble for the factories . . .
 No skiving now, the whistle blows . . .
 All present and correct . . . they know
 There's now no safety net, that's what they need
 That's monetarism, Nit . . . are you agreed?
NIT: Yes, m'lady, I dare say there's truth in that . . .
PIMP: Too bloody true, what . . .! Lazy scum!
 Can't wait to strike at any turn
 Been spoilt, what!, by the Welfare State
 When what they desperately need is a swift
 Kick up the ass mate.
MAGGOT: That's all very well, you know,
 But the barometer of fate

Has placed us in the opinion polls
Behind the scummy Socialist crud
Behind old stinking 'Feet' we limp
While you just drag your foot
Old 'Feet' just stumbles on and bleats
Like some old flasher on Hampstead Heath.

PIMP: About this invasion my lady . . .

MAGGOT: Shut up a mo' . . . I'm thinking hard . . .

PIMP: Of course, of course, what action to take?

MAGGOT: No! Whether to fry it in butter or lard!

PIMP: Oh myself, I like my bacon grilled . . .
A few tomatoes sizzling there
Bung in a mushroom or two
And if you've time then just prepare
Two slices of fried bread, that's a treat
Or if you like two scrambled eggs
Quick whipped and fluffy like molten gold
Coffee steaming from fresh ground beans
. . . That's my definition of ecstasy . . .

MAGGOT: You're wasted as Foreign Secretary
Your talent there is hardly used
We need a decent bloody chef
The Commons kitchen's the place for you!
(Aside.) *Ah! I have it . . . I have it Nit!*

NIT: Yes, my lady, what have you got?
Have you come up with some inspired plot?

MAGGOT: I'll make a Spanish omelette!
At first I'll crack some Argy eggs
Throw in some tasty British herbs
Well flavoured with strong English earth
Then, round and round the cauldron go
In the poisoned entrails throw
Hate and good old Tory guile
Plots to cover up our sins
Lies and slander to beguile
Then throw massive outrage in,
Synthetic will do just as well.

162

To make the mixture rise and swell
Then add more than one thousand dead
Tears of children's salty brine
Broken hearts and widows pining
Mothers mourning for their lost boys,
Collect those dewdrops to make the paste
Soldiers' howls as they lay burning,
Throw in the lot and keep it turning
Olé, your Spanish omelette!

PIMP: But who will eat this foul stew?
MAGGOT: The entire British press, you fool!

The *Conqueror*

SAILORS' SONG

Rule Britannia, Britannia rules the waves
Britain never never never shall be slaves.
We've spent twelve thousand million quid
On our defence in twelve short months
And now you see money well spent
We'll give a demo of our strength
We've got the class and discipline
The training, thank you at your expense,
Communications are next to none
Weapon locating radar-chum
We're on our way from Scotland's shores
Until we reach the battle zone
We're going fast beneath the deep
On our way to the Argy Fleet
Attracting curious sharks and whales
Who cannot believe this giant fish
That slides armed with its deadly eggs
That will be laid when we will mate
War's just another way to fornicate
We'll fuck their slaggy Argy ships
Action stations, we'll rehearse a hit.

SAILOR 3: Dear Sheila, just cleaning my gun
    I tell you it's great . . . it's just fun
    We're not going to kill anyone
    We're just keeping the Argy on the run.

SAILOR 4: Dear Rita, we crossed the Equator today
    It weren't half hot, the guys sunbathed
    We'll be there in about a week
    We're safe as houses and the roof don't leak.

SAILOR 5: Dear Doreen, I feel so proud my love
    To be part of this great Fleet
    A hundred and seven ships on the way
    And each man will say . . . 'I was there that day.'

SAILOR 6: Dear Mum, I can tell you I'm scared
    Don't know what we're facing down here
    It's so quiet beneath the surface and still
    But each night we can watch a film.

SAILOR 7: Dear Dad, it's getting colder as we close in
    The South Atlantic's cold as ice
    I can't imagine what it's like
    If we had to bloody swim.

SAILOR 8: We're told there's now a TEZ,
    Total Exclusion Zone I mean,
    If we find enemy ships within
    Then we can blow them to smithereens.

SAILOR 9: Dear Judy, I don't want to kill
    In fact of war I've had enough
    The Zone we're told's two hundred miles
    So they'll stay out, unless they're tired of life.

COMMAND: Two-hundred-mile Exclusion Zone
    So if the buggers stay outside
    All we can do is be like cops
    And whack them if they stray across.
    Still I'm not sentimental, this is war
    The Argies began it, but I've no hate
    But I wouldn't half like it if they want to play
    I've got a lovely bunch of coconuts . . . called Mark 8.

Argentina v. Britain

PRESIDENT OF ARGENTINA: No, we don't wish to fight no more.
    It's a question of principle that's all
    We have to settle this old score . . .
    The Malvinas belong to us
    It's on our continental shelf
    It's part of our long history
    You have no contracts sealed and signed
    You came in 1833 and stole
    What was rightfully our land
    We never sold it to you
    We never gave it to you
    So please give it back thank you
    We tried so many times to call
    To ask you when and how and why
    You put us off, we're foreign scum
    You ignore the warning signs
    'End colonialism in all its forms'
    Resolution 2065 . . .
    The United Nations wrote that line
    Nineteen hundred and sixty-five
    For seventeen more long years we wait
    And get nothing . . . nothing at all
    You would not even negotiate
    What did you do for your Malvinas
    Nothing, but bleed it, suck it dry,
    We supplied the Islands' needs . . .
    You gave nothing, nothing at all,
    Oh yes, perhaps a little greed . . .
PIMP: All right, old chap, now settle down
    Don't get your knickers in a twist,
    History is made by time
    And in that case you must believe
    The Falkland Islands really mine
    Or rather ours, sorry slip of the tongue,
    You cannot separate the strands of memory

Who's right, who's wrong . . .
'Prescription' is the word that I would choose
Defined in our good dictionary
As, 'a claim founded upon much use'
We've had our good old British stock
For so many long winter years
Toil the earth and break the rocks,
And backs as well with sweat and tears,
It's just a little piece of England now
So be a good chap and piss off
Or else we'll blow you to kingdom come.
You know we're on the way old boy
So why don't you just scuttle off
And show your boss that we mean biz,
OK? There's a lot of muscle on the way
He'll understand that there's no deal,
Just stay put in Argy land
I know it's tough, inflation's high
Five hundred per cent and going up
Wages are low, your debt is huge,
But . . . don't use the Falklands for your subterfuge.

CHORUS: Oh for a brace of Exocet missiles
That would ascend the brightest heaven of invention
The sky would be their stage
Super Etendard jets to fly
Six hundred and eighty miles per hour above the waves
The deadly Exocet once it is launched
Cannot be stopped until it strikes
Since radar with its seeing eyes
Can only read what's in the sky
Below ten feet its eyes are blind
Oh who would know the cunning fiends
Had fixed them to their flying wings
We did not dream nor could not know
The bastards had such weaponry
This flying spear of death is quick

You can't shoot down an Exocet
When hurled above the choppy seas
You don't see it till you are hit!

Cabinet

MAGGOT: Well done, Pimp, the bastards know
    What follows as the night the day
    If they won't move, those junta creeps,
    That Britain won't just watch and pray
    And see our Islands given away . . .

PIMP: I told the bugger, it's up to him
    The message could not be more plain
    I spelt it out, withdraw or else
    The answer could be a lot of pain.

MAGGOT: You're sure we're quite prepared, my Nit,
    No fuck-ups now, no tricky biz
    The press has swallowed all that shit
    And the country's right behind us too.

PIMP: Yes, my lady, we're nearly there
    And your speech yesterday when you compared
    Yourself to Churchill was a wiz.
    Hitler's very useful in time like this.

MAGGOT: Never mind all that, just give us facts
    We must be certain we will win
    Not land our boys into the fat
    Because you screwed up, you nit.

NIT: We're all prepared, the Yanks are there
    We will know when it's time to hit
    Old Cowpoke's loaned the electronic toys
    We can even hear them take a shit.

MAGGOT: Spare me your squalid anal jokes
    Your public schoolboy legacy, Nit!

NIT: Yes ma'am . . . sorreeeeee!

MAGGOT: What about those bloody Exocets
    Those rotten greedy French have flogged
    The French are not averse to deals that stank

They'll climb down sewers to make a franc.

NIT: It's all arranged, they'll spill the beans
And tell us the secret of those stinging bees
The intimate details, how fast how high
And how easy it will be to swat them from the sky
We have no need to worry ma'am
We know all they can hurl at us
An inventory you might say
The French have been a good ally.

MAGGOT: How long, how long before our arm
Can swat you might say, with our might?

NIT: Three weeks is all we need, three weeks
And then we'll be right there on sight.

MAGGOT: OK, Pimp, here's the plan, unplug your ears
For three weeks then you show restraint
Talk peace, remonstrate the wrongs,
Make amends, negotiate, discuss
The pros and cons, offer a plan . . .
A waiting time before it's time to go,
'Time please' we go out gently from
The pub with easy and all friendly smiles
The landlord must lock up the doors
And so like us he will away
Into the night, we had our day
And quaffed down our pint
Just look after our good folk
Perhaps a golden handshake and Amen.

PIMP: Oh goody then there'll be no war!
Just threaten and then make a deal
A long lease back, divide the oil?
The Islanders can go to hell.

MAGGOT: No, Pimp, you rotten little turnip
You greasy stupid dotty sod . . .
That's what they'll *think* – why divvy up?
When we can have it all . . .
If we let UNO back in,
Sit down for weeks with Garlic Chops

Debate our terms with the gangster mob
We'll look like we've been shat upon.
We're not a third power yet you know
We've got some balls in the old bird yet
Though I doubt the pair of you
Have got much there to boast about
If we decided to talk to them . . .
To negotiate with those we hate?!
Then goodbye Tory Party from the land.
We're two per cent behind the Reds,
That's all we need to show how weak
And spineless we are to old 'Feet'
They'll shit on us from a great height
Can you see Feet in Downing Street?
Because we couldn't make the pace?
Besides I don't intend to move,
I just redecorated the bloody place.

CHORUS: Around the land, in every pub,
In every dining room and lounge
The voice of England can be heard
Discussing the Falklands with angry sounds
As if the family jewels had been thieved.
Outraged. The telly on, the pot of tea
Refuelling parched throats for verbal war
You'd never believe until last week
They didn't know Falklands from Leigh-on-Sea.

The Commons

MAGGOT: We didn't know, no, not a thing.
Bolt from the blue . . . I couldn't believe . . .
There we were eating their meat,
Enjoying West-End musicals inspired by their chiefs,
How does it go? It's really quite sweet
'Don't cry for me, Argentina'
We were shocked, shocked we were . . .
You know it's quite a strain

We weren't prepared, no ships, no planes,
Not a dicky bird was said . . .
If only they had asked us nicely . . .
Said, 'Please Maggot, can we have our Island
Back', polite and quietly,
We would have considered, I would have said,
'Piss off, you greasy fascist pigs'
(Cheers.)
'Go screw your mother, you filthy wogs'
(Cheers.)
'You want to put your dirty toe
Upon our cropped-lawned island home.
You've got some hope, don't make me laugh
Or I'll shove the junta up your ass!'
(Cheers.)

FEET: The Labour Party now demands
That we avenge this bloody deed
For bloody bloomin' bleeding war
Should we declare right now, no less
Foul and brutal aggression must not succeed,
Labour's not a pack of Tory weeds,
We'd be there, yes damn right we would.
What happened to 'Intelligence', they all dead?
Fingers up your assholes, blind dumb and deaf?
They've been telling us for years
They're going to give the mighty boot
What have you been doing love
Fiddling the books? Or plotting
With asslicker Nit, or Pimp the pontz, the crooks.
(Boos.)

SIR FISH FACE: I think we should ban Argentina
From entering the soccer World Cup.
(Cheers, 'Piss off', etc.)

NIT: I take great exception to Cheesy Feet
Accusing us of dragging our foot
When we were never even warned
Or if we were we didn't hear . . .

170

FO didn't tell us or the post went astray,
The lines were bad I believe that day,
Or else, oh yes we were away . . .
The file got buried or got mislaid
Oh, then we were on holiday . . .
Yes I remember that, the weather was fine . . .
You know how memos pile up high . . .
We did write a letter, I remember that . . .
But forgot to send it . . . The last chap was a prat.
But you know what we do with prats
Or silly buggers who make a balls,
We give the bastards the bloody sack
And they sleep it off in the House of Lords.
Anyway who are you to talk
In your worn-out elbows and smelly cords?!
You march against the nuclear bomb! (Shame, shame.')
I've seen you stride with long-haired poofs
All the way to Aldermaston! ('Disgusting!')

MAGGOT: Can you imagine old Feet in the shop
When we'd come back to check the stock
He'd have the whole damn country in shock!
('Bravo!' Cheers!)

REASON: Surely, before we shed young blood
We must seek an ointment for the wound.
To heal must be then paramount
No more killing, not quite so soon
('Bollacks', 'Appeaser', 'Coward', etc.)
There must be time, no blood's been shed
Not one young English life's been lost
You seek a medicine for the sore
Not hack it with a bloody knife.
All human flesh belongs to God
You take one life, you take the world
Did Jesus say, 'Throw your stones first,
Those who are innocent of any sin.'
('Balls', 'Rubbish', 'Coward', 'Appeaser'.)
The world's become a tinder-box

You set a match and watch it flare
Death has become a TV screen
That we watch from our soft armchairs
('Sit down', 'Piss off', 'Left-wing pontz'.)
If you can call yourself Christians
If you believe in Christ our Lord
Then you will seek the bloodless way
Not solve it with a flaming sword.
('Commie', 'Bollacks,' etc.)

The *Conqueror*

SAILOR 1: Dear Janet, love, we're there, it's cold
We do six-hour shifts, I'm bored
Scotland lost the match we hear
There's not much else I can report.

SAILOR 2: Dear Sheila, still cleaning my gun
I'd love a decent cup of tea
Or even read the daily *Sun*,
You know, we still ain't killed anyone.

SAILOR 3: Dear Rita, there's not much about
We saw a couple of old freights
A sitting duck . . . but couldn't shoot
The sods were outside the TEZ.

SAILOR 4: Dear Doreen, still feeling so proud
But I can't wait to see their ships
It's dark and silent as the grave
I'm dying for us to make a hit.

SAILOR 5: Dear Mum, we don't know what's going on
We hear no news except the crap
They send us from HQ at home
And politicians' daily chat.

SAILOR 6: Dear Judy, I don't want to kill
I can't imagine what it's like
The waves are like giant hills
The sub feels like a block of ice.

COMMAND: Two-hundred-mile Exclusion Zone

A lot of bloody bollacks that
To steam around and watch the buggers
Stick their tongues out, safe and fat,
Hold on, we've had a signal here
'Go out and sink a bloody ship'
'Which one?' 'Who cares, just something near
You've got to make a bloody hit'
There's nothing in our target now!
'The other sub will make the kill'?
Give us a chance, we'll look around
We'll get some juicy Argy ship
Chock full of arms and fighting men.
'Westminster wants some action' . . . Shit
We've got our hands tied by the law.
Can we attack them from the rear
When they're outside the lines *you* draw?
That just ain't cricket, is it dear?
Or they may say, and it will be true,
Britain does not rule the waves
She simply waives the bloody rules!
Wait, hold on . . . just hang about
I'm picking up a distant tune
Let's go to periscope depth and peek . . .
A silhouette against the moon . . .

PIMP: (On phone) Hello, hello, Maggot, that you?
And how are things at home, my dear?
I'm chatting up old Cowboy Joe
And it could be that peace is very near.
MAGGOT: Hello, Pimp, speak up you drip
And don't believe all that you hear
Those greasy wogs are cunning sods
With all their talk of peace plans now
That our Task Force is bloody there.
PIMP: Well, to spell it out, the sods agreed,
Immediate cease fire, number one . . .
And then withdraw all Argy troops . . .

That's what we want to flaming hear
A third party to govern it,
While we thrash out conflicting views
And then the Islanders to have a say
Before the final solution day . . .
Well, it's not bad, is it, what d'ya think?

MAGGOT: What do I think . . .? It bloody stinks
Who cares about the rotten Islanders!
It's not what this is all about,
You stupid simpering silly pontz.
You think the wishes of those few
Will dictate how and what we do
We're not negotiating with them
It's us, Great bloody Britain mate
It's our corn that they stepped upon
You think we're going to war for them?
Spending four million quid a day
For eighteen hundred Bills and Ben!

PIMP: I know, I know, but still they say
Their wishes will be . . . etc. . . . .
And they can make peace this very day
It's up to us, they've cleared the decks
What shall I say ma'am . . .
Can I say . . . yes?

MAGGOT: No, no, no, no, no and no!
And that does not quite spell out yes.

PIMP: But ma'am, they have agreed our points . . .
Old Cowboy's flogged himself to death
We've been up all night . . .
For nearly a week . . .
A hot line between Joe and them . . .
We've squeezed the best possible deal . . .
Squeeze any more the marrow is next . . .
Give them a morsel . . .
Don't put it to the test . . .
They'll withdraw . . . we've won
Talk terms . . . no blood behind a desk . . .

MAGGOT: Tell Cowboy Joe, I need a fight
    He needs it too, expose the sore
    That may spread inside the flanks
    Of England if we have no war
    There's twenty-eight thousand Brits
    On whom the world's eyes hold in awe
    Are we going now to turn around,
    Say, 'Sorry, lads, false alarm'?
    Tell Cowboy, if we do then, farewell,
    England falls to Socialist claws
    Who will tear our land apart
    Then who will support his Cruise missiles
    Planted like teeth in our fair land
    To scare off the Russian Bear
    Or bite any invading hand?

PIMP: But then we're nearly almost there . . .!
    What can I say then when they ask
    What did your old Iron Lady think
    Of our strong plan we made for peace?

MAGGOT: Stop whining, you sickening spineless wimp,
    Oh God if only I had men around
    And not this pair of leaking drips
    That dribble daily in my mind.
    Tell Cowboy I support *his* wars
    Prop up *his* Nicaragua
    Ignore his murder squads he sends
    To clean up vile El Salvador
    So screw this pissy peace plan, Pimp!

PIMP: OK . . . I see the danger, ma'am . . .
    The troops return . . . the drooping flags
    No 'knees up, Mother Brown' in pubs
    Or clinking glasses in Buck House
    No medals, no heroes lined up . . .
    Before the Nation's TV screens
    No celebration of the deed
    That spells out British victory
    No revenge for the filthy slur

No hands in mouths waiting for news
No photos in the *Daily Muck*
Of Tommies clambering up hills
With smiling faces, British flags
Atop a craggy mount . . .
No Islanders with whoops and cries
And cream teas for the hungry lads
Wide-angle lens of history
Being made by Fleet Street hacks
Who follow us with hungry lens
Ready to frame for all the world
The conquered lying in the dust
And Maggot Scratcher raised up high
And then, vote Tory . . . written in the sky.

MAGGOT: A teardrop now steals from my eye
Oh, Pimp, for once you now speak true
At last, you see the truth at last
At long last you must see our cause
Thank God, the scales fell from your eye
You see, we must defend the state,
Not just some piece of rock with sheep
Dropping their rotund turds so thick
Or gentle Islanders shedding wool
Or rocking chairs for weary feet.
It's England, now at last you scan
The breadth of history . . . The pulse
Of England must be strong, we *must*
Punish those who commit wrong . . .
You know we've got them beat,
We paid the deposit . . . Let's just complete.

PIMP: So what shall I tell Cowboy Joe?
They're sewing up the peace plan now.

MAGGOT: Say you couldn't get through,
You know the phones are always bad
By then we'll scuttle their little 'plan'
But make up a tale for the man.
(She hangs up.)

PIMP: Now I shall have to lie *again*
    She always leaves me in the shit!
    Oh well, it's nothing really new
    Not when you're taught by the master bitch.
    (Into phone) Hello Joe, how are you and how's the wife?
    Listen, I can't get through right now
    Nobody home, and embassies are closed . . .
    Weekends, you know, nobody works . . .
    Yes, the plan seemed fine to me
    A hiccup perhaps just on one word?
    What word is that they want to change . . .?
    'Wishes' . . . to 'Aspirations' on the clause . . .
    Oh well, I'll have to call HQ
    To see if 'aspirations' now will do
    I know it's only just one word,
    I know that time is running out
    But we must analyse the sound . . .
    Weigh it carefully on the scales
    Make sure we have value for a pound
    I'll call you back without delay
    OK? . . . and, er . . . have a nice day.

CHORUS: Now you see and now you don't
    Imagine pounding on the rocks
    A score of Harriers now unleashed
    Shredding their targets like angry hawks
    Then sweeping into the sky
    Dissolving in a womb of cloud
    Only the deep and throaty sound
    Is heard as it again prepares
    And down down it dives
    Ploughing up earth rocks and trees
    And sending fear into our enemy
    Who cower, trembling hair on end
    Affrighted by this show of strength
    Watch them as their spines will bend
    Beneath the blast of British breath

Hot, fierce as raging angry lion
Protecting her young cubs from death.

Lunch at Chequers

MAGGOT: We've not much time, the sands are running out
  And at the end we'll be checkmate
  By compromise and deals, my friends,
  Unless we give the most almighty clout.
TELL: (Off, the war) Damn it all, we're hitting the buggers hard
  All day we rained down great dollops of pain
  We attacked again and yet again
  Port Stanley never will look quite the same
  Our chaps are doing all they can but
  If the buggers stay outside the line
  The boxing match is fought with gloves,
  Let's get them off and get some knuckles
  Cracking on the swine . . .
WOODY: Hear bloody hear . . . What! Bloody shame
  I call it . . . sod it, let's clout the buggers
  As you say, knock one off and they'll not
  Come out to play another day . . .
MAGGOT: Trouble is they have accepted all our terms
  The very minimum we would accept,
  They have by now accepted, bar one word
  One bloody word will be the straw
  To break the camel's back. That word
  Will not go down, not if we choose
  Not to accept their peace-meal stew.
  But once they inform Joe that it's on
  We can't then change our minds and say
  It's off . . . Can we . . . How say you, Tell?
TELL: Bloody hell, that's what I bloody say
  Damned good lamb New Zealand eh!
  That's it . . . buy British or nearly . . . tasty . . . what!
MAGGOT: Have some mint sauce, Tell . . . Yes can we

Say it's off? I mean, can we say, sod off!
Too late, the balloon's gone up?

WOODY: Smash the buggers, in or out the bloody Zone
Reclaim what's ours, if we don't we'll be
A right example to the rest, besides
We could then test our toys, warn Russia too,
We'll make an example of all those that
Think the Lion is just a sleeping cat
I'm dying to see how Sea-cat missiles
Fare and Tiger-fish torpedoes blasting
Holes, at half-a-million quid a time,
Bit costly that, but think of all the orders
We will get once they see them in the act
Tests and war games aren't the same
As seeing them work on living game.

TELL: Right, let's get to work, let's heat it up.

MAGGOT: Oh Tell, you speak the words I want to hear
Where can we clout the sods before they
Crawl behind the UN skirts in fear?

TELL: Sink a bloody Argy ship!
Hit them where it hurts the most
A packed full, well armed with young men,
A thousand maybe more, hit in one below
Condemn to darkness their young pride
Then watch them cave in when they feel our punch
You take one out, you take them all
They'll be on their knees, you'll see.

MAGGOT: Oh Tell, I'm thrilled with ecstasy
More lamb? Go on, it's piping hot
Some roast, 'fraid they're just overdone,
Now go on. . . . sink one!? Bloody hell.
Then it's all over really? You think so, Tell?

TELL: Could be very well . . . They'll see
That we mean business . . . won't risk
Coming out and lose an arm, maybe a leg
We've got them well and truly pegged.

MAGGOT: They wouldn't attack *our* ships, would they, Tell?
TELL: Can't see how, we know their strength
    Got all the facts, thanks to old Joe
    Who fed us all the info that we need
    To know, give us the word, let's go.
MAGGOT: You don't need me, just do your work
    I'm right behind you lads you know.
WOODY: We've trailed a lovely Argy ship
    Stacked full as Tell has just described
    We've got them in our sights . . . could
    Blast them now to kingdom come.
    One battleship just steaming on
    With two destroyers by her side
    Like taking two alsatians for a walk,
    They'll bark a bit maybe
    But won't do much when they will see
    Their master's bleeding guts,
    But then they're just outside the TEZ.
    Please change the rules and then you'll see,
    Madam, a swift sharp British victory.
MAGGOT: Can we do that? So easily.
    Or won't it seem in the world's eyes
    That we have been a mite extreme?
WOODY: No, bloody hell, let's say we saw them
    Start to stray across the line . . .
TELL: They posed a threat to us, our boys,
    Were steaming straight just hours away
    We had to sink the bugger without delay!
WOODY: They're bristling with fire power ma'am,
    With two missile-packed escort destroyers
    Like armed guards ready to defend the boss
    Who himself carries fifteen six-inch guns.
    We had to sink it or face our loss
    God knows how many lives we'll save.
MAGGOT: You think we'll save lives?
WOODY: Of course, we'll stop the war
    They'll have no bottle left to fight!

TELL: Attack them now, before they go,
    There may not be a chance again
    And then we'll bite our nails and sigh
    Oh why didn't we do it then, you'll moan.

MAGGOT: What do you mean, 'before they go'?

TELL: Well . . . info is, that they're heading back home
    They're on a track you see, two-ninety degrees,
    Between ten and eleven knots, we'll lose them
    Though we've had them in our sights
    A day or more, we're waiting for the light.

MAGGOT: Sunlight?

TELL: No green, give us the green one, madam!

MAGGOT: I may say, now forgive me if I winge
    That to sink a bloody ship (sailing away
    You say) in cold blood gives me just a twinge
    I know it's right, I know . . . but when I think
    Of hundreds of young boys, they could be ours,
    Stopped dead and floating in the drink
    It does . . . just for a second . . . make me think . . .

TELL: Don't! . . . ma'am don't, be hard as steel
    The Iron Lady, come, not brass not tin
    Like leaking oil can in *Wizard of Oz*,
    But iron! Rigid, hard, inflexible . . .
    Your reputation earned the whole world wide
    The Iron Lady with a velvet glove??
    No! Iron fist to match a steely heart.

MAGGOT: (Inspired) Then sink the bloody sod, that's what I say
    We'll change the engagements rules . . . OK.

TELL: We'll drink to that.

WOODY: Can't wait to give the bloody orders
    They will be pleased, they're getting
    Bored sailing around the endless seas.

MAGGOT: What shall we say? Let's all decide
    To tell the same story, on the day.

TELL: Get Nit . . . to extricate his tongue
    With due respect from out your ass,
    And tell the press and parliament . . .

'A heavily armed surface attack group
Close to the Exclusion Zone, was closing
In on our Task Force . . . only hours away . . .
Ignore them at our peril,' that's what he'll say.

MAGGOT: But that's not strictly true, they're sailing away
You say, some forty miles south-west of the Zone
Can't we sink something deep inside . . .
That we can certainly justify . . .

TELL: There's bugger all . . . They've kept outside
And this one's closest, ma'am, and soon
That won't be there much longer . . .
Look, if we don't hit it now
We'll have to sink them in their ports
And claim we heard them start their engines
And posed a threat to our Task Force!
And how do you know that they
Won't turn . . . How do you know it ain't
One big bluff . . . They calm us down
And then one night ka-blam and blast
And British lads are feeding sharks.

MAGGOT: Those last words indeed touched my heart
Of course my woman's soul trembled a jot
At thoughts of bloody bodies
All unseamed and torn apart
And widowed mothers clutching their
Now fatherless sons and daughters
Must admit since our wombs carry flesh
And blood and watch the shoot become a plant
Must admit that for a moment I did hesitate
Forgot that I was iron, instead a mum
Worried when child is late . . .
What's the time?

WOODY: It's one o'clock

MAGGOT: (Recovering) Then give the order . . . Let it be swift.
Anyway those bastards started it
Let them now take the consequence . . .

CHORUS: Now cast your mind o'er wind-swept choppy seas
    Where ships lay waiting rocking to and fro
    A great armada, armed with might and men
    Who wait, alert, primed ready to unleash
    The power that is awesome coiled within
    Imagine now the crew. Some sleeping, some awake
    Their radar scanning thunderous clouds,
    Some writing letters home to their sweethearts
    And others still deciphering strange codes
    Which spell the fate of those who live or die,
    Some playing cards, some singing old pop songs
    While others dream of clutching their warm wives
    And in those cloudy seconds between sleep and wake
    Imagine they will turn around and hold their mate.
    For some, alas, this night will be their last
    Their young unfinished lives will be reclaimed
    Within the freezing sea, their unknown graves.

The *Conqueror*

COMMAND: Up periscope . . . OK, we see them clear
    Action station . . . all at high alert
    It's nearly fifteen hundred hours, Sunday May the Second.
    That's nearly seven o'clock back home
    Opening time in all the pubs
    We'd wander down and have a pint
    Maybe play a game of darts or two
    I've got her in my sights, ten thousand tons
    Of steel, at least one thousand Argy men
    Just slowly ploughing up the sea
    A steady speed of ten to thirteen knots,
    Like some old carthorse pulling reins of foam
    But at her side two dangerous chaperons
    Ready to destroy with claws
    That reach into the sky some twenty miles
    Seek out your heart and then like bloodhounds
    Hold your course until they taste your meat.

SAILOR: They're only blokes like us . . . don't fire . . .
    Not fire one off . . . like in cold blood . . .
    Not warn 'em first and fire a warning shot?
    Like shift over boys, you're getting close
    It's not the Second World War . . . is it?
COMMAND: We're now four thousand yards away from her
    Portside and steering the same course
    A wicked sea and choppy waves
    Some four or five metres high and fog,
    Standby and fire one off . . . OK . . .
    We'll use Mark-8 torpedoes, they're safe
    Dependable, and should get there on the day.
SAILOR: The wind's now blowing fifty knots
    Across the raging, icy sea . . .
    To put a man alive in that
    Would quietly send him first to sleep
    A few more minutes he might live
    Dreaming in his icy bed
    Until the cold has drained his heart
    And death sucks out his last breath.
COMMAND: Fire one. Forty-three seconds it should take.
SAILOR: God . . . Let them not feel any pain . . .!
    Oh Jesus Christ . . .

(Silence of forty seconds. A sea of anxious faces. One
face in pain. Will it hit?)

COMMAND: . . . A hit! . . .

(Total cheering . . . back slapping . . . One man still frozen
in his agony . . . Sounds die out, just the faces
moving in celebration. Slow fade.)

CHORUS: The first torpedo pierced the ship like
    It was made of butter – sunk right through
    Then tore inward and upward through
    Four steel thick decks . . . It spun its deadly

Groove . . . It sunk itself into its guts
And ripped its soul apart . . . The old ship
Then simply turned around and died . . .
The lights went out . . . just silence . . .

(Darkness . . .)

Dead men were everywhere, in bits.
A piece of arm and here a leg . . .
Upon the deck a figure covered in burning oil
All black and running as the heat roasted
His flesh. Three hundred and thirty sailors died at once . . .
The others dragged their shredded flesh
To rafts to face the icy sea, thirty-six hours more
Or less . . . The conscripts, boys of eighteen years
Stayed disciplined and kept their nerve
Each one ready to sacrifice himself to
Help an ally or a wounded friend. At
Seventeen O one just one hour more. The *Belgrano*
Sank stern first beneath the waves.
SAILOR: The dead men did not pay the price
Of peace, for others died the selfsame
Way, when two days later in revenge
Our ships were sunk, and many died
Or were simply burned alive . . .
SAILOR: Somebody threw the first stone
When the *Belgrano* was going home.

(On screen the following image: 'I would do it again' . . .
Margaret Thatcher. Blackout.)

MASSAGE

CHARACTERS

DAD
MUM
MAN

AUTHOR'S NOTE

Massage is just another investigation into one of those delightful phenomena of the British way of life along with Wimpy bars, Boots the Chemist, the corner pub, Chinese take-away, chicken tandoori and the newspaper shop, all vying for attention in your average street and round the corner the latest, although not so new, Massage Parlour where your average bloke goes and gets what is endearingly called 'relief', being a simple wank aided by some viscous lubricant. 'Relief' is a choice epithet to describe the British way of sex as if the male had a painful itch or wound and needed some medical aid. The play is a bit of fun with the concept of the massage parlour as the sanctuary for men who come tormented and distraught and are sent away renewed by the dextrous hands of the woman who then reveals herself as a truly liberated female, having to deal with what would appear to be almost a sub-species of the human race, the male. Her role is the stronger of the two since she wields the power and is the possessor of the means of the relief!

No holds are barred in this sexual comedy since I wished to write something deeply erotic, pornographic and obscene as an exercise is the aesthetics of this counter-culture. In the end, by freeing language, I felt that the play ceased to be a dirty play since it is open and reveals itself without deviousness or guile . . . I have yet to perform this piece but hope to some day, although the present climate of sexual fear and political correctness may see its innocent message warped and wilfully misunderstood.

DAD: Simple-minded jerks and fuckwits / mouths agape and crutch on fire / wiggle ass and 'love you's dripping out their stupid lips / while rock and rolling down the grotty disco / dressed like freaks that from your worst of nightmares grew living flesh and blood / but there the semblance ends / for they to us are like to chalk and cheese / to life and death / from wholesome *Homo sapiens* to thing that from a womb wast nuked and came out like the devil had distributed his evil seed within / I saw one strolling down our natural homely street / our strip of sanctuary lined with trees and turds of dogs so neatly dropped / with wholesome pub on corner / saw this thing as if from outer space / hair spiked like porcupines / and he thick wedged in shoes totters his hair pinned nose into our suburb haven / brains of ants / they follow the dull parade of clones / the dyed and painted saboteurs of all that's holy / the wreck of our permissive state zipped out on grass and smack / and I don't mean a romp in epping forest with your favourite tart for a taste of slap and tickle but the shit they shove into their empty skulls / so roomy that it needs the constant kick of noxious dope to prove that to itself it's still alive.

MUM: More tea, Frank?

DAD: Yeah, pour out the nectar sweet balm and elixir / the tonic for our dried-up british throats / the balm that greets our tired morning eyes / when rising from our stinking pits in balham, kent or palmers green / prepare ourselves for one more day of shirk and strike / the brown and steaming stew doth reinvigorate our will / stiffen our pride and puts the sparkle back in our jaundiced eyes / that magic brew / that simple british leaf / that greets us late at night before thick slumber wraps us up / a fag just puffed before / put out the light and then put out your light / oh! the bubble gurgles and it glob glob globules out the old brown pot / that heart-rending and happy sight / old browny on the table top / the pride of england / ne'er feel the stroke of bitter loss or strife while cuppas will be there to dull the razor's edge / and as I say farewell to this fair state / let my last taste of england be /

a nice old brown and sweetened cup a tea / (drinks).
Bleedin' hell . . . it's bloody cold, mate!

In massage parlour

MUM: So many years have passed since first I found a way to
honest toil by doing what I like, that is to squeeze the miles
of cock that sausage-like have passed between these walls / so
many cocks so many shapes / some large / some small / some
tall and thin have strutted and have heaved their silver pearls
upon this well-worn slab / they stand up to attention, ready
and alert and pass themselves to me, in trust that I will shed
their load and send them out into the world all light and
fresh / and ready now to face the thing in semi-detached
bliss / with me their fantasies are now fulfilled / I am the
shepherdess that tends the sheep / and milks the cows, for
that is how it seems / pour out and squeeze the nectar and the
pain / I'll rent my hand and voice / my subtle touch to their
world-weary aching ends of flesh / just aided by the finest oil /
I baste their swollen joint, caress and soothe, tickle and
pinch and faster now and faster doth my hand like a
pneumatic pump explore the riches down and bore and drill
until the hit. The target, solid gold / bull's eye, then whoosh /
the spray ascends as showers on an april morn / some kleenex
doth remove the clues then off they go these valiant and most
noble men of england / to return to their dull wives with sour
miens / their nagging and unwholesome shrill / who frame
their dried-up lips into a ring of woe and pour the doldrum,
poison and demands of married life / that rings and contracts
they believe have given them /

MAN: (Stripping) Oh woe is me let me escape and be soft putty in
your hands / I cast myself like ulysses when he, the sirens'
filthy sound did drive him total mad / give me a massage,
sherry, if that's your name and make it topless now as well.

MUM: For topless as you know another fiver must be paid / plus
fiver for relief / oil or powder / choice is yours / or take the
total lot / be bold the day is yours / invest another ten and I

will shed my briefs / those gossamer sweet drawers and shall arise like venus striding forth / naked as the day / you'll have me quivering there as succulent as aphrodite and guileful as the sphinx / my hands will touch you like you never knew / you'll writhe like quicksilver between my flesh / I am the virtuoso of the wank but lest you should be tempted and ten pounds more at that / there is a treat in store which I reserve for only those I like / the special crest of all the rest / the summit and the peak to make your very bones cry out and shriek /

MAN: Pray gentle nymph / thou sweet and foul / thou noxious temptress in these cells of red / tell me thou devil what treasure might I avail myself without being cleaned of all my pence and save a buck or two / so that my kids at school might feed and not face hunger by my lustful greed /

MUM: Fear not my gentleman nor seek high favours at low cost by sentimental guile / with chatter of the hardship and the face of little kids to float with pinched and hungry face before my woman's eyes / I know these cool male tricks to make a score with chicks with cheap words forged in heat and lust, and not be paid the price for my soft woman's paradise / the cost is high / if you cannot afford then stay at home with tv on and pine / watch your old mate undress to bed / and as your eyes do scan that worn-out wreck / those gnarled legs and ass spread out to bust and think yuk no sweet thrill but only wasted life ahead /

MAN: O honest whore / those words that trickle from your oral, smart and lash me with the stings of truth / I pay much more to keep the shriek at home whose constant open mouth *keeps* wolf at door / plus two fat bonny brats which tho' I love, between the three of them, they suck the life from out my craw.

MUM: What does she do for you? Does she caress you like I do? Does she anoint your prick with oil that's precious and perfumed in shades of musk to make it glisten like a rain-lashed oak or carved by michelangelo all gnarled and swollen / knotted and thick proud with mushroom head glutted in blood the rich red ruby racing rampant to the crest / transporting lust to the nerve centre of it all / the emperor of the body / the stalwart rising beast / the hungry eyeless mouth / the snake about to spit / straining at the leash above two mighty balls rich and filled up / those oysters primed and ready to give up their dewy pearls / I, me my woman's sting / my soft electric thing I fantasize in you to make such hard-ons as you never knew you had / I live to make you glad / that god shoved on your end this whisper shred of flesh / this toy / this morsel that the more you eat / the more it grows in solid hunky meat /

MAN: (Dawning) Aah! So there's the treat!

MUM: A mouthful of deep throat
You'll be a dog in heat
(She takes it out and performs it.)

Home

DAD: What can I say as I return to this soft womb / the triumph of my years of slog / and view upon the coloured screen the wonders of the human race / and as the old bird dishes up the magic of her cordon bleu I slosh it down with half a pint to take away the taste of mush / my cock sits all quite comfortable and small at peace and smiling in his sable sack / digesting pleasure from the afternoon when like a tiger sprung he from his slack and concertina'ed shell to march forth into action . . . all pell-mell / she sucked me like a good'un just to tell you straight / my life felt like the source of it was drawn and slid along the tunnel of love, my prick / it was the rocket ship that made its vertical ascent and soared upwards to heaven / my piece of red-hot rocket stood alert on pad / fuelled up for scorching take off / octane blast / all tight and proud / come on and press that magic switch / the button that would send us spitting into space / would send the plume all white and shining into orbit / at last as if my flesh was inside out and raw / as if some fruit was peeled exposing succulently its juicy meat / I felt the tremor start like acres

down and deep / in the inferno where the ache is dim, deep
down in the abyss where chasms stretch and mountains
crack / where rocks begin to seethe and boil / and lava bakes
just aching to escape and pour into the air its bottled boiling
snakes of white-hot lust / so there I was / it cost a bundle /
topless, bottomless too / I had the lot / the works / the oil and
french or gobble at the end / straining at the leash / buttocks
compressed almost to billiard balls / I turned myself like
inside out / and then like mount vesuvius started to spout /

MUM: More tea, love . . .?

DAD: But hush, here is the thing from whom I hide the best part
of my sting . . .

Yeah, throw some in and bung us too some holy ghost that I
might then anoint with perfumed marmalade the crusty
bread and wash it down with magic rosy lee . . . nice tea . . .
(Praise.)

Job Satisfaction

MUM: Last night I had a busy time I tossed off seven was fucked
by three / and gave head to two more / so tired but satisfied
with work / my old man in armchair all well and truly smug
at home, in bliss with kids the shiny offspring of our
connubial lust, tho' lately his once almighty hard-on has hit
the dust / which to tell true has been some small relief to a
girl who is all day engaged in giving same at work called 'on
the game' / tho' game it hardly is / more like a slog to get
through the assembly line of dirty dogs.

Legal Whoring

MUM: So you who scorn and look askance/you opened up your
legs when first you saw your mystery as capital / and made
yourself into a painted bait to catch the slippery eel / my cunt
and woman's touch it's true I sell but you would not give all
until you were provided with the means of living well! You
ensnared your men and threw your golden lassoo in the air /

but first you saw the lucre in the bank / the sexual capitalist would tease and goad / say not now darling, later on / would pout and be all coy in lacy frills / glossy lips and soft perfume in rolling hills / would lie in wait tarantula to catch her prey and milk him slowly / that's your way.

You lived in quilted eiderdowns and china sets / a bedroom spare for passing friends / a dog called captain runs amok among the old man's shirts and sox / you so faithfully daily wash / you lucky bitch / for treasure lines your flock-lined walls / your tasteful three-piece suite in lounge and rocking chair for the old man / a ton of babies' things to wash which stink / au pair bungs it in wash machine / the dryer too / oh super darling . . . ain't she cute / your baby's sweet / she's only two / samantha . . . oh that's lovely / shit! She pissed all over my best suit / the garden's coming on this year / we're growing pansies and freesias dear / you playing bridge this afternoon / oh no, today the kids come home from school / I love the white brocade / the lacy curtains look so fresh and frothy / don't, captain! Get out in the garden / samantha! Don't you give the dog a hard-on / leave him dear / I know it's pink / oh shit, the cat's shit in the sink / brr! brr! It's mum, yes I'm ok I just don't know what to cook today / he's getting bored / what shall I make / I know he works hard . . . 'Evening dear' . . . a peck and then the gin appears / nice day darling . . . 'not too bad' I'm bored to death / it's just like dad and mum when I was young / the same desireless dreary death and boredom dandruff and bad breath / is this the life / is this for me / you chose it dear / you held the key / to puss in bank and made him pay if he was to unlock your safe / you wannit then you work and say / my pussy's sold not given away a ring a house a signed contract / he sweats and every day he will regret / he's bored / tough tits mister / pay you wretch / she's whored her arse to you you git / you loved it once / you're bored right now / too bad pal / you're stuck to the cow you wanna scram? It'll cost you dear / she'll suck your money better than she ever ate the thing that got you into trouble mate! She'll drain you / look she's good at it / she's just a high-class whore you git / she steals from men and makes them pay whenever she gives puss away / she does it legal like and smiles in church while ma and pa cry like two jerks.

The British Way of Life

DAD: I'm up / I am the british worker bred from the holy lineal strain / the viking and the dane have put the good old british rich blood in our veins / we fought and smashed the filthy hun / painted the world red coast to coast / from zanzibar to taj mahal / the pucker sahib was master there / we taught the darkies who's the boss / erased the aboriginal and tossed the black man back into his shanty town to make south africa a jewelled crown / we showed the pakkies how to play a game of cricket the english way the world we made a safer place for christians and our wives to saunter in / and showed them jesus, taught them sin / and watched the millions come pouring in / and I mean pounds not bleeding wogs / not stinking krauts or dirty frogs / but good hard british notes / a pound was worth a pound in them good days / nowadays inflation runs so fast / you're running like diarrhoea flows out your arse / in case you shit your wages out before you've time to buy a snout / before you said hey! twenty smokes it's up again / before you've time to nosh your grub, so mum and I we wolf it down whenever we go into town / in case the waiter comes on strong and says hey mate your steak's gone up / it's one quid more than when you stepped inside the door / in olden days an indian was just a darkie in a big wigwam / but now the high street chimes with names like taj mahjal and tandoori / with eastern star and bengali / the mob have come across to sink the nation in a stink of pancake rolls and popadoms / hot curries that can make you shit from islington to oxford street / the mob have come to take revenge and take this island back with them / they'll stuff us full of curry that one day just one almighty fart will blow away this septic isle / we'll float in seas like some almighty turd you sometimes see bobbing its little head in the wine-dark sea / whole streets and boroughs pound with drums and cassette decks the size of tanks they'd carry on their shoulders like a little kid you'd give a ride / they look like blackened martians skating down with earphone stuck around their frizzy crown / it's dangerous now to step outside / in your own manor lest you collide with king kong doing fifty miles an hour. Put the telly on, love / I'd love to see old farty licking arses clean of some old has-been celebrity.

The Whore's Story or One's Story

MUM: I scanned the western world for cock that gallops at a lifted frock / we know it fades / 'tis temporary / that's why we add the touch of lie / with cream and powder / pout in pink / coyly resist in satin and stink of musk behind the ears / and make them think we're little dears / small pussies cradled in white pants as soft as marshmallows and tame those hot red monsters out for game / but cock must be attached to rocks that sparkle / rock-hard stocks and shares in bank / securities and no small wanker out to use us for his selfish gain / our box is assets / truly stored we are the sexual overlords / the sexual capitalists of the world / so whore and housewife are the same / they both go out to work for gain / the one in hard cash for quick time / the other will wait until what's yours is mine. *Come to me*, come to *me*, you men of rock whose thighs are weighted down with balls so heavy under-used and bored / come to me at massage house / and let my hand play out a tune / that on your flute will make you swoon / and if you want the topless too / and special bottomless as well, a tenner more will see the sight that men would die for / rot in hell even to glimpse / the shining tips and ornaments / the swelling vales and creamy sponge of silky breasts and as I plunge your cock into my mouth, my tongue will round your head enfurl and part my standing legs for you to dip your hungry hands into / I'll squirm and wiggle, pulse and twist /

I'll bite your steaming bulging prick / I'll take it deep down far inside my throat / I'll chew it softly tender, stroke with oil the smouldering shaft and lick the veins in the underhalf, running my tongue along its ridge / dip the tip into the cyclops eye / while far below you crush and scoop my creamy cerements / my holy fruit my pomegranates / ripe raw figs, your fingers squeeze my slit and dig / dig down, dig deep dig far as if to rip the fruit from off its branch / and then I squeeze your thickened shaft caress your swollen balls and sense the pulse begin to start / the heavy blood-swelled prick grows to its final ramrod juicy stick / the spunk begins to rise / my mouth goes faster faster now / the knob inflates its crest like some huge flower opened up / your fingers still like snakes dart in and out and crawl inside my silky satin mouse / oh yes the flood hot thick and white bursts through the tunnel in fiery wet hot sticky spouts / in gooey creamy bursts / the gates break / the flood aches through / in spurts of warm soft silvery glue / oh comey gurgle gulp and slurp / hmmm! hmmm! . . . swallow hot vats of semen down and lick it clean / while up above your face, serene like now the moon was free from clouds / and smiled with silly cheesy grin / meanwhile I felt it shrink again and small like going back to its cocoon / he gets up, smiles and y-fronts he puts on / he reckons he's had a tasty one / I send him out into the world all nice for wifey / stroked and spoiled / was that all right ducky? . . . 'yeah great' his old lady at home would hate to do the things I do / would say I'm just a filthy whore / but her old man comes back for more /

Transactions

MAN enters massage parlour.

MUM: Hello, ducky / seen the menu?
      Hand relief . . . ten quid.

MAN: Oh yeah.

MUM: Topless relief. Fifteen quid.

MAN: Oh yeah.

MUM: Top- and bottomless, twenty quid.

MAN: Oh yeah.

MUM: French twenty-five and full french thirty.

MAN: Oh yeah.

MUM: Spanish thirty and greek forty.

MAN: Oh yeah.

MUM: Greek and french forty-five.

MAN: Oh yeah.

MUM: All-in fifty.

MAN: Oh yeah.

MUM: Reverse, greek and french fifty-five.

MAN: Mmm.

MUM: Reverse, greek, french and spanish, plus bondage seventy.

MAN: Mmm . . . what's spanish?

MUM: Between the boobs, dear.

MAN: And excuse me, but greek?

MUM: Anal love, love.

MAN: What's french then?

MUM: Oral.

MAN: And full french?

MUM: Oral and cum in the mouth, dear.

MAN: I see.

MUM: All right, dear . . . what would you like?

MAN: Tell you what . . . I'd like a touch of spanish and a slice of greek and then spring into a double reverse with a piece of french easin' off into a whisper of bondage / a grab of relief and relax into bottomless sex whip out into greek and ending in a full french at the end.

MUM: I can't do that, can't go from greek to french / I can go from french to greek or you could have a two-girl bottomless-topless hand relief into bondage. A bit of tv french and whip down into greek finishing up at athens.

MAN: Ok. I'll have that. How much?

MUM: A hundred pounds all-in but I'll do it for fifty.

MAN: Ok. I paid my gelt and went into a dark red room / my flies were bursting in anticipation and I sunk into my reveries as I undid my pants / I stood in my knickers with my great

sausage squashed tight and making it stiffer, I looked in the
mirror and thought it quite nice as I heard muzak trickling
through the flock-lined walls / there was kleenex in the
wastebin, I unpeeled my pants and out it sprang like a hoop
or like a greyhound sniffing around for meat and wondering
what to do . . .

Whore's Life

MUM: Do you think I like my cunt used like a sink / a vile cesspit /
a bin of stink / a crock of rotting sperm-choked drain /
repository for all the pain of man who comes so stupid in
with breath of rot and yellow grin / who stumbles over in the
dark, his alcoholic brain in nerve-torn shreds / the last bits in
the lower self / the basement of his mind / let's have a fuck /
he sees a picture in the shit-heap room he occupies of tits and
panties black / stockings held up by straps and open thighs
and arse to clutch / he sees the morbid tattered pictures in his
head when boredom, drunken conscious stunned only a
walking thing that lives to eat and fuck and sometimes shit / a
thing that staggers out at night with mates dead equal in
thick leer and hate of women, soft things animals and tears /
and hate of love, people, earth and fears only that his cock /
his filthy smegma tip won't stand up when his money's out /
his heaving bloated corpse / his rotten evil smell / this junk of
man / this piece of evil hell / still tries to get it up / still farts
and burps 'oh fuck it, love, I can't get stiff . . . I think I
boozed too much, oh shit . . . it's gone again, just hang about
tell me some filthy stories to make it stiff and sprout' / ok. I
tell him about whips and frightened teenagers well bound
with leather straps / legs spread with downy dewy thatch /
whose tears flood down and beg and cry / yet burn between
their virgin mounds / for fingers, tongues and hard thick
pricks to pound / she moans oh no! soft rosebud tits / small
even slits he pulls apart / opens up the rose petals and peers
inside the flower's heart / its stamens and its pollen exposed
to the lurid eye / so whip the soft pink creature make her

squeal / her soft pink arsehole makes you thrill and bend her
over like an animal / examine all her sacred bits / explore each
part that once forbid and secret in the sanctuary of the shy /
your cock grows fat by weaker creature's pain / the more it
hurts the greater is your gain / you are now hero / conqueror
and proud / your prick runs rampant now and stiff the magic
elixir for dick is kicking others / so hit and pinch / slap hard
and whip / her eyes they open wide and beg no more but this
is sweet for you and then the thick hard shaft slides in the
juicy glue and howl scream cry / oh god these sounds are
paradise while down below the furnace is ablaze / your filthy
dick's on fire now and shoots its steaming spunk along the
trail / and shrivel slurp and slop / wipe off / 'that's great,
ta-da' / you and your stink you gather up / open the door and
into the night's old womb you're swallowed up and join the
stream of human filth that teems along the gutter swill /

MAN: (Still waiting in parlour) So there I was / all waiting in my
rose-hued room and cock as white and hard as marble / when
I thought of all the lips and eyes and tits and thighs and all
the sighs when hands clenched in the back row of john
garfield's body and soul and shy to touch the crushy blouse
whose swollen promontory housed within the stiffened bra
the marshmallow and squeezy tits with orbs so pink and
delicate that sneaked out when your hand would clutch the
melting snow and nipples sweet would peep between your
fingers / saw her knickers when in armchair's squelchy
throne her knees so high and eyes would dive down to those
svelte and mossy thighs / the inside of those legs / whose
stockings clasped like lizards' skins and fire glowing in the
grate / would wonder as I glimpsed the ivory veil / that
masked the heavy squelchy mass of sticky schoolboy dream /
the pouring lovesick ecstasy / the juicy runny fruit / the
cocky cunt / the figgy rasp of hissy snaky pungent hole / I
would so calmly lift the gentle dress and wait for her to stop
my filth caress / just wanted now so much my hand to glide
right up to where the heat and scent and fantasy collide and
knees and squeeze and higher yet and no, her hand has

censored nothing. Still I slide now each new inch my itch-
hard hungry fingers scale the slope, another pulse of blood
pours in my prick to service what it hopes will be a fast
insertion into ecstasy / above the tongue twists round and
now one sucks and now one rolls the pink wet carpet out /
she nibbles tip of tongue and close tight eyes whose lashes
like thin spiders' legs crawl out her sweet mince pies and
still / yet still within the thunderstroke of drum pound heart /
my hand still scales the warm silk soft and creamy leg until
just at the end of stocking felt the flesh the narrow channel
separating leg and crutch and was a pearly bridge I scanned /
oh sweet the heavy pound of blood / my heart withstands the
heavy thump / the furious flow / I kiss the harder, flooding
mouth and lips with all the flesh my face can separate from
skull as if by some osmosis we conjoined or rocks whose
atoms smashed into each other's grip and now for all time are
fixed / and so her lips and mine were right entwined who
knows where hers began or where did mine / and then yes
then the arched embrace / her head pulled back / the other
hand / rings her cotton waist / the other like a filthy snake /
dress now gathered up in folds like ripples from a stone-
pierced lake / so my hand was there along the slippery vale /
towards the honey of her soul / her squeezy triangle of joy /
and soon so soon I'd feel my fingers sense the pertinent and
thin silk ridge / and yes I'm holding harder yes I'm near / my
heart is flood in blood so red hot current thick and then yes
then / her crutch seemed almost now to lose itself to me and
slide towards my hand / my hand becomes my soul / my
hunger, my antennae to my lusts and greedy musts / is like a
taste or tongue / my hand becomes a stomach / starved and
hunger struck, and then yes then / just then, just when I was
so near and felt the heat / and sensed the peaty rich and
swollen sack / my hand and fingers traced its path / inch by
inch / until my fingers were in touch with velvet ambrosia
and prick-hungry lust / my hand then knew the end and
beginning / knew that gold was there and waiting to be
mined / I felt my hand open and close around the gift / a

sparrow settled in my hand / and then like dream and ecstasy
was in my palm which bore the sweet stigmata of her love /
my fingers became snakes burrowing beneath the gauze / did
lift the veil so tight and yet just room enough / I pulled it
back as if peeling a skin and felt my fingers like hot knives
into butter sink / and so my fingers sank deep down and
drank like sponges parched and gasping for her touch of soft
underbellies of squids or persimmons that break and crush
open when ripe and squirt the too sweet juice into your bite /
MUM: (Enters.) Hallo, love . . . day-dreaming?

    I do not ask for guts hung down in tresses bobbing in the
bubbly waves / I like my pricks hung stiff like some upright
and young spring rose / not shrivelled in a heap / cut off at
root by missile bullet or knife / you who squeal at this and yet
condone the rats that chew upon your babies' limbs / the rats
that carry plague of hate / the filthy death's head shrieking
death to all / so all may be as dead as they / hate walks in
petticoats and skirts just as easily as khaki blood-stained
trews / hate stems from thick black bile that's boiled in
witches' stew / round the cauldron we will go / pour in
frustration / dried-up cunt that for a score of years was
parched / and withered prick that died unused and crushed
between pinstripe and office seat / balls hung like prunes or
mouldy figs / throw in that too / and to repression's smelly
breath to season it / and then mean withered fingers that
never knew the soft caress / no never felt the ache of sex / no
never sweetened soft and pulpy parts with awesome gift of
life that pours from out the stem of love's caress / throw in
the pot small wizened eyes that have the hate of basilisks /
that hates the naked sight of god's pure fruit / the living
flesh / pop in those fishy eyes and stir until it's thick and
rich / then add now the viper's tongue / the bitter lashing
whip of scorn / prejudice and hate / intolerance and greed to
make this rot concoction into a rancid paste / tongue that
ne'er knew peaceful balm of love or sounds to pour oil on the
troubled seas / tongue that drinks from casks of wrath and
spews out drivel shit and waste / words so vile like sink and

shoot to kill / attack revenge / how dare you / splatter /
tongues that consign young and brilliant downy boys to be
drowning in blood and burning oil / if everyman's your son
and brother / father too / how could you make your heap of
evil stew you crock of filth / if you knew how a soft caress
could calm and make the temple that you occupy god-filled,
how would you then give words / orders to kill except you
never knew / numb withered eyeless / senses buried in hard
crusts of scarry tissue / leathern worn out / living at the end
of life / the barest light from deadened batteries / so pour in
all to make this soup of death / a mass of tangled limbs tossed
in the bloody foam-flecked sea / my child and yours sinking
down deep in gore / were it yours / were it yours / you filthy
evil coward rot-gutted insult to a whore /

The Nature of Dirt

DAD: Oh that made a change from all the filth outpouring from
my filthy gob / let's rather read the sunday press / regale
ourselves with the minds of yobs / who talk more shit than
ever was / flushed down my loo in the name of wit / let's cast
my mind to other realms / like strolling down a country lane
and pick bluebells in velvet woods and feel the wind caress
my brain / see fairies dancing on a brook where sunlight hits
the rippling waves / should like to hike down endless roads /
where summer paints a golden haze / nor feel the end will
ever come / like those hot youthful endless days / so strolling
through the blackberries and scratch my knees on thorny
pricks and clutching wordsworth tenderly I lay beside a
tickling brook / I felt the grass caress my neck / saw mighty
branches float and sway / as if by indian eunuchs they were
fanned to brush the blowflies from my face / I lay and
thought tho' half asleep I heard the wind whisper sweet
things / saw dancing pair of butterflies dissolve like
snowflakes in the sky / which poured beneath my lazy lids /
all blue then purple as thick sleep poured over me in
summer's heat / an aching slumber fell and gently folded me

into its spell / I sank like stardust in the sea / or like a pebble thrown so eagerly by some small urchin / hits the wave so hard and shatters crystal spray and then slowly it sinks away so sank I 'neath the sound of bells from distant steeple / odd squawks / the ripple of a brook would talk and distantly in summer haze some thrilling laughter blazed a pathway to my hideaway / yet through the deep veil of my doze heard sweet young schoolgirls far away rejoice in school-work's end of day / the bells I heard chimed four the magic hour that all children score upon their hearts for years / the teatime, four when all england stops / forgets their fears lays their hammer and their chisel down / even the hangman stops / and says not now my friend / the noose will wait / the surgeon deep inside the brain to brilliantly remove the source of pain / he too will nevertheless stop and pause as he see the theatre clock strike four /

Down tools, down instruments / the nation breaks as if to say, this special time of day we pray together / gently sip the golden brew and know from queen to pauper up and down the state this hot leaf will remove constraints / dissolve the walls / we'll drink together, rich and poor / a nice old english cup of char / I lay there so contented on my green and silken bed and realized o wretch that I alone in the vast tapestry of england's patchwork quilt / a little emblem stitched within its hills / will not be there in village teashop / sanctuary / or even greasy alf's café / to celebrate with all mankind / to be the vital link that binds the souls of england / hold the teacup trembling to my lips / close my eyes and taste sweet bliss / but this was not to be / so I lay back letting the slumber dull the ache of quenching that old taste I had and soon forgot / the voices grew and then I as I was midway through oneiric land and like endymion to sleep forever on his little grassy bank / deep in my dreams or so it seemed to me / I saw a vision slowly walk in schoolgirl tilted hat and thick pigtails / all glowing nubile and so virile, strong and bursting out their bodies like a song to nature / their cotton blouses bulged apart and pearly buttons seemed to pop as if like young

spring roses could not be restrained from opening their
petals to nature's gaze / their brown and tawny thighs like
some great scythe cut through late summer's grass, knee
high / they slashed their way leaving a trace of giggles hung
upon the day / just like the wake rude ships upon the emerald
green do make / so deep down in my hypnos cave / my lids
stitched down and fast asleep I dared not try to wake lest this
be just a dream and fast dissolve in glare of day / 'cause
dreams are sweet little things that come to tease you with the
things you dare not do or cannot have / the things you
fantasize about / would love to take into the upper air but
cannot do and dare not make / lest real world squeals do
break your bones as they turn you on the prejudicial wheels /
but casting these dull thoughts aside which like cold showers
before sun can render its hot beams the sweeter and more
rich when rain has gone / now, came upon my ears some
cracking twigs proclaiming this dream's not all mist / I
scarcely breathed knew not if dream or bold reality stunned
my brain / I cared not but still fastened lids and dreamy
globes did rise and fall inside my inner universe oblivious to
all except the sound which closer grew / I screwed all my
attention to its source like radar scan and now the sound was
caught inside my web was scrutinized inspected by taut
nerves that stretched to catch the very air caught on the
breath / and now sweet thin and piping words hung on my
web like fireflies / mere traces / nothing clear but now I hear a
sound like 'oh helen let's sit here' / helen! so I even knew the
name of one . . . the intimate clue could call the sound and
know its magic would respond inside her sweet ear and make
her turn her face to where I lay / heart pounding like tarquin
before lucrece's rape /

So down they sat while I in grass so tall did spy, and heard
their giggling sounds add yet more music to the air so thick
in warble chirp and wind that whistles through my secret
lair / they came to make love to the sun and shed their girly
weeds upon the bank / oh hot I was and thrilled to view this
yet delightful early morning dew / this unripe rose this

unpicked fruit / so just as if to catch the warm and rampant
sunrays 'tween their thighs she paused, chin cupped in hands
as if in clouds of schoolgirls' dreamy thoughts / while down
below the bulging sun did play his golden fingers o'er her
cunt / and my eye did send a ray of light to snare in the sweet
open air her sight / of cupid sweetened and unblemished
white / her shining schoolgirl flag / which now with idle fingers
underwaist she scooped unpeeling like a second skin does
from a snake / and up she lifts her smooth curvaceous bum /
two full moons rising as the knickers slide down and one leg at
a time is eased from silky cotton fantasies of schoolboys'
listless classroom dreams / her small soft crest / her tender
mouse was clinging on between the marble columns of her
house / and then behold she lay down on the green and dewy
bank / eyes closed against the heaven's piercing eye / and then
I saw her very flanks unfold reveal the choice part of her
thighs / they seemed to glisten in the light fresh haze of
summer's bee-droned endless days between a slender tulip or,
like a peapod opened fresh or velvet petals of some flower all
hungry for the sun's warm shafts to ooze its yellow molten
thru' its heart / it opens slowly now to face the trickling hot
rays from the sun's embrace / 'oh lovely now' she sighs and
gurgles in falsetto rippling flute, 'if only now . . .' and this I
can't believe but heard the words bruise past my ear / heard
them detonate loud and clear with . . . 'if only now I had a
man's silk prick all would be fine / a big and juicy horn to play
with' / 'hmmm' her friend agrees 'a thick hard juicy prick to
stick in here . . .' when even now the thought draws one small
tear to weep for joy between my thighs and from my throat big
lusty sighs / I pinched myself in disbelief is this a fantasy or
wicked dream sent by the devil in cunning jest that has you
grasping out for snatch / your arms around some luscious girl
and then just as you're to drink your fill awake rudely to mum
in curls / but no, 'twas not a dream / not even when like sirens'
sighing on the wine-dark seas did try to lure poor ulysses / they
played and frolicked endlessly / thrusting their fingers like five
keen slaves ready to obey her every whim / they danced and

played sweet lusty tunes upon her soft and aching quim /

'O fuck me,' one was saying now, 'o lovely man please fuck
my lovely burning cunt / it's hot and runny dripping for a big
thick slice of horny pan' / their eyes were closed tight in their
trance so self-inflicted by sweet lust / the child not broken in or
satisfied by hot young roughs / so sadly they must fantasize
until some young pink prick gives them their fill / my tool by
now was like a greyhound in the trap bursting to escape and
pour its sap upon those open flowers / whose honey spilled so
wastefully on the grass / so trembling I undid my bursting
flies / I was all thumbs but out it sprung and reared its head /
its knob all big and angry red, ready to spit its load and quench
the fire down below / where those two sweet urchins did
moan / so stealthily and not to fright I crawled through the
long grass to where the sight and smell did draw my swelling
beast and now half swooning in the summer's heat / I could
almost reach out and touch their feet / the air stood still and
hung so heavy in the perfumed auburn summer and late
afternoon while shadows crawled like inky stains / I crept
snake-like upon these maids who writhed like thrashing waves
beneath a storm-lashed sky / imagine there I was, just framed
in space on hands and knees / my cock a trumpet leading on or
like the cannon loaded to heave its lead upon the enemy's
head / then suddenly as if just on the crest of some great
mountain peak / the child seemed to have reached / for now
her face broke in a smile and shrieked out in her joy o god o
god it's there / I heard the rapture in her voice make shock
waves in the english teatime air / I thought 'tis now / just
follow where your cock will thrive / go in and say hallo! it's
good to be alive / my penis swollen aching to be let loose /
dragging me like some great stallion on its way to home will
start to canter when it sniffs familiar roads / so now in twitches
jumps and starts / I'm ready, can't hold back, I'm home at
last / the birds did stop eyes watch / even the wind, it seemed
to drop / when suddenly in that split second beheld by
thousands, insects, moles and birds. Each keen to see the rite
performed that has gone on since life on earth unfurled / when

in that second / cock on fire / a pearl worn on the blind eye of my love / or like my cock did shed a tear in sheer relief to quench at last this biting thirsty beast / so in that second held in time / all silent / golden warm and air like wine / so just then / just in that split second / thighs all tense like springs ready to pounce / so just then in that same second she awoke and screamed 'oh fuck helen here's a dirty bloke' . . . / her shrieks tore from the air the fine embroidery / the great design that had with care been sewn / each stitch to lead to the great masterpiece / the final act not yet wove in / like the great masters saving for the end the *coup de grâce* to relish all the more the sweetness of the central core / the burning motive from which all else provides the background score / so watched I now with grief the stitches torn apart and dropped / the canvas smeared the story ripped in two to be rewrote / and gazed in sadness as I watched the two dissolve in dust shook up by rushing schoolgirl feet and dumbly contemplated my puzzled and now shrinking meat /

The day was grey now clouds had stamped themselves across the day with muddy hobnailed boots / but still thin piercing beams did struggle and did spill some yellow paint upon a lonely daffodil / I tramped home low in spirit and in cock / the dream that came to life dissolved as if 'twas pierced and stabbed with bloody knife / my head ablaze decided to avenge the lust that raged within my groin / so off to local sauna / high street cheam / the first time that I had to my local been / I thought it wiser not to be seen by evil eyes / this town is full of dreary spies that love to identify a figure's disappearing back and them to say didn't I see you in the high street sauna the other day / but now my caution's thrown about like some great schooner on the rampant seas that seeks a harbour anywhere just for some peace /

MUM: Another day of blissful graft / have a nice day love / 'twas good to see the men of england going home all happy to their tea / no more will infants feel the bloody kick / nor mother nurse a blackened eye since jack and albert, jeff and fred will be released in cock and head and be all peaceful, like before the set [tv] and chortle at the football / go to bed / a quiet fart under eiderdown, g'night love / up and down the breadth of royal england from noble prince to dustman bill / turn out the light luv echoes still, from voices all content with secret thrill from furtive hour with their local whore / I've had them all pop in their joints for basting / from blue blood cock all white and thin / stuttering as he tried to stick it in to giant darkie whose protuberance precedes his owner by five mins at least / we need then two rooms to receive the roll of flesh before it shrinks / so now home to my joe / but hush there is the bell / I suppose I can accommodate one last seminal spill:

DAD: I hope she's nice.

MUM: (Not recognizing him in the dark) Hallo, duckie you're just in time / not seen you before / oil or powder what's your choice / come sweetheart now where's your voice / you've gone a little shy / now that's ok / relax we'll make it go away /

DAD: (Aside) *Ye gods / I dare not look around but those words that emanate from out that gob sound like my old lady / oh ye gods / it can't be / shit and piss and throw in arseholes too / she sounds the same as maureen does / oh cruel fate to torment me like this / I am undone oh bollocks cocks and tits /*

MUM: (Dawning) *Hold on now, maureen, but that back with spotted bum like roses in a field of snow or raisins in some porridgey scum looks all familiar like old joe's / that voice was gruff and tired like joe once home from day of selfless graft he'd flop into armchair and burp all happy then to be indoors with glass of guinness and familiar moan!*

DAD: *Oh canker, oh rash of tosspots but that smell / those hands with soft and quishy squeeze seem by me to have been seen in other places like and shall I guess / washing up dishes in our old nest / oh cock and arsenal spurs as well / bobby charlton throw in the lot / I'd trade to get me out of this hell spot.*

MUM: *Oh fuck and sausages that turn to snakes oh blast of hell that now within my gut awakes the writhing serpent grawing / now undone the trick has been found out / the tide of money that flowed with spunk / like ease has now washed back with acid bite and cobra's lash /*

DAD: *Oh god / let the floor open and swallow me / whole like jonah was by the mighty whale / and then spat out in some new place where she could never see my face / my shame inscribed my habit exposed with trousers down / no teeming hard-on now but shrunken rose /*

MUM: *Aye, 'tis ture / my old man wandered in no doubt informed by some vile snooping lout some bastard perchance strolling in informed him that I work in sin or so they call it / those that take advantage / those that sneak off in a secret hour for subtle flick of wrist or hire of flower that ignites those parts that other wives fail to reach / they have informed on me / those dirty beasts /*

DAD: *Hang on, before my shame and guilt take hold as doth a noose to hang me high / then what's my old lady doing looking spry in panties frothed with lace and naked thighs / the dirty whore who now for some time didst say goodnight with parting kiss / roll over with a face all creased in bliss / so this is where the filthy whore did dwell / my wife was milking cocks in this red-lighted stinking pit of hell / oh farewell peace / oh farewell joy / my wife's dear precious cunt was just for all the world a thing to use their toy!*

MUM: (Deciding to come clean) Hallo love / what you doing here? doth come to spy your wife I fear / some nasty turds have spun some foul and horrid verbs inside your ear / all right the game's up / I confess it's true / what next / divorce or shame / so kick me out / you've caught me on the game /

DAD: [Aside] *Thank god she thinks I only came to spy / I did not know my trouble and strife / my darling wife was in the market of open flies / but she believes in blameless quest / I came to discover this hornets' nest / this darkened hell hole of the pumping wrist / and oh my precious mary's mixed up in this / I'll be an actor . . .* You filthy slag! you dirty whore / I could not believe of those that told me what goes on behind this door / my darling wife has flogged her rose / my flower / my ornament of joy / my sceptre / my own doughnut the furry cup that slaked my toy when it was thirsty dipping in and stirring up all innocent the muck that's in this bin of sin / my little mouse / my winking puss / that's probably seen the cocks of half the town / that's tossed its sheckles into your greasy pockets / oh rage / oh slimy mildewed canker / lukewarm tea / choirs on telly / pubs closed

at three / the rolling stones and vera lynn / oh curses high and
foul on thee / take thatcher powell even benn / I curse on thee
that lot of them!

MUM: Oh how your words do thrash like whips and cut my heart
and soul to bits / my husband ne'er again will lay his head /
all snoring in our precious bed / who needs the cash the filthy
dough when in the end your karma knows and throws it back
like hailstones hard and sharp / it tears the veil perfumed but
thin / the stinking lard comes thru' and foul corruption too /
but know my sweet I did it for us both to line our future with
some easy dough / but gave some comfort on the way / to
those who at the end of slog in factory and pit have no sweet
mate to take the ache and pain from it /

DAD: How foul you toad / you whore / who knows now oh god!
maybe I'm carrying some obnoxious sore / that's slowly
eating away poor me /

MUM: No sweet fear not / their weapons always were well
sheathed / no never was abused I swear / and checked by
doctor / everywhere who vouchsafed my purity and health / I
would not don't you fear conceal by subterfuge deceit and
stealth some canker that would eat away *your* health /

DAD: O god / o shatterer of souls / o blinding light / remove from
me this awful sight / let me escape from seedy pit where
snakes unroll their foul spit and suck down good old high
street air which is like nectar or ambrosia compared to this
unwholesome lair /

MUM: Forgive me, frank / give me a chance / I'll give up / never
more to swing a leg or wrist to make pneumatic dance / the
money, let it rot and stink /

DAD: (Aside) *Now hang about / let's not excite our wrath / we're out the
storm, I'm safe in harbour / do not bite the hand that feeds / the
horn of plenty she has tapped . . . or squeezed / why throw it out /*
(To her) So what's it all about?

MUM: What . . .?

DAD: I mean like I can understand . . . / you need a little more
than I / can rustle up in weekly skive /

MUM: No, I will give it up / will never more I swear joe / I will work in woolies' [woolworths'] or elsewhere / if you will have me back / oh joe I'm on the rack / I'll scrub floors / anything to take the sting from being just a whore /

DAD: You make a bundle every week.

MUM: I make enough to make our future sweet /

DAD: You'll bring it home and split it you and me.

MUM: You mean to say . . .

DAD: (Emotionally) Why give up such lucrative pay?

MUM: Oh joe, you'll be a pimp!

DAD: Who cares / who wants to save and scrimp / now I'm getting over the first shock / I now admire / no talk of sin / free enterprise / there's gold in cock / we have to adjust now to the times / and morals are ok for those who can afford to be so wise / but us who get screwed every day / by boss then state who drains our pay / are not so bound to legal graft / when others thieve and rob / aye there's the rub for who would bear the whips when there's a fortune to be made in pricks / so doll I say I do forgive your ways /

MUM: Oh joe / I'm overcome with joy / we'll be a partnership you'll see / toys I'll buy that will delight all free from grubby tax collectors' greed / and when our fortune's made a house in sunny spain and swim and bake /

DAD: Sounds good to me / so love I do forgive and beg of thee / since I am here and to tell true am slightly turned on by your gear / if you would donate free my dear / one of your samples for a treat / I'm feeling like a dog in heat /

MUM: Of course my love / it's been some time since you have wished a dip in mine /

DAD: Must be the atmosphere or role / for now I must confess / I find you rather *more* exotic now I see my wife's a whore /

MUM: Oh joe, you've made me proud / I'll give you what you ever dreamed / unleash your fantasies to me and I'll give you the best you'll see / describe the innermost dark secrets of your soul / your bestial cravings / anything goes!

DAD: Er . . . I think I'll have relief today . . . with topless too, if that's ok?

(Blackout.)

LUNCH

CHARACTERS

MAN
WOMAN

AUTHOR'S NOTE

Two people meet on a bench in a park near the sea. It could be anywhere. The man sells the most humiliating item of uselessness that he could find to foist on to the public . . . space. He sells space in one of those cheap magazines that nobody has ever heard of. I did this once. The magazine would put the names of established and famous firms inside their pages to convince the innocent small printers and tradesmen to buy a half page. I trundled round Stoke Newington with the papers and forms in my briefcase. It was a good old life. I lasted one day. So naturally I used this experience to describe my growing awareness of the space in my own life and this profession seemed an apt metaphor for the male who is hollow and tries to give himself to the woman, who quickly realises the void within him but not altogether void. It's filled with the debris of expected performance, vanity, shallowness and sexual exploitation. Through their mutual catharsis the man learns how easy it is to be honest and reveal himself and how painless it is to do so since we are all afraid of revealing some shallowness we are convinced is at the bottom of all our good intentions.

Lunch was first performed on 19 December 1983 at the King's Head, London. The cast was as follows:

MAN	Ian Hastings
WOMAN	Linda Marlowe
Director	Linda Marlowe
Designer	Linda Marlowe

Empty space bathed in a cool white light – faint music being played –
strange discords which italicize the action from time to time. A beach
anywhere. A WOMAN *sits by a table, she is facing the sea, a deserted*
beach café. MAN *enters frame from left to right. He sees her –*
enormous reaction – freezes. He seems unsure whether to come or go.
So just stares.

She senses him behind her – they hover thus for a moment, she
aware, still, eyes chasing from left to right.

He, as if to pounce – stealthy, but still, eyes boring into her – two
animals caught in each other's fear. He edges forward as if casually,
carrying a briefcase.

MAN: (*Aside*) Beautiful, oh she's beautiful – who is she waiting for
– no one for me –? Her neck soft as a baby's thigh – I could
bite valleys out of it. I could . . .

WOMAN: (*Aside*) Turn around . . . ? No, that's an invitation – who
is he – throbbing silently as a shadow behind me – burning
holes in my back.

MAN: (*Aside*) To go up to her – gently slide up like a ghost . . .
kiss the nape of her neck – then she'd murmur softly – soft as
bees and offer her mouth to me like a hungry bird.

WOMAN: Poor beast . . . he's dumb . . .

MAN: Hungry bird . . . mouth open . . .

WOMAN: Shy – he wants to – talk – he should . . . (*Turns her head
quickly.*)

MAN: (*Startled*) Right through me she looked . . . straight through
me . . . I didn't exist . . . I was a tree.

WOMAN: He could . . . he should . . . his mouth . . . aches to
speak . . .

MAN: JAWS LOCKED! . . . TONGUE ROOTED INTO MY MOUTH . . .
granite . . . speak now, or remain mute . . . dumbstruck . . .
Dead
(WOMAN *moves as if to leave.*)
No, no not yet! Budge not thy heavenly bum . . . petal-lined,
proud, strutting . . . Not yet . . . Heat-filled bitch of a
thousand juices! Not yet.

WOMAN: Too late . . . too late, soon . . . Quickly!

MAN: Walk past . . . casually sit . . . Speak! Shout!? No, I'll go away . . . coward . . . Oh, you terrible priapic coward – cock hard . . . gut soft . . . coward.

WOMAN: I can't say anything . . . can I?

MAN: Too late – too late – the heart aches – the shock would be too great.

WOMAN: A pity – he was nice.
(*She has begun – so she must go.*)

MAN: What words ensnare? – captivate – enchant – rape – suggest – amuse – interest – stun . . . (*To her*) Lovely day!

WOMAN: Yes – yes it is really lovely!

MAN: So many lovely days we're having – all at once.

WOMAN: Suddenly . . .

MAN: You would think it could be summer.

WOMAN: You would think so.

MAN: Yes we're lucky.

WOMAN: Certainly we are.

MAN: Do you mind? (*Seat.*)

WOMAN: Please do.
(*They briskly examine each other.*)

Alternate:

MAN: Blue eyes nice – I like that – fullness in lips, soft . . . skin smell, legs crossed, skirt short . . . darker recesses leading to the various succubi and incubi swarming in her panties, those gardens of cotton roses, a child wandering through hot gardens . . . those smelling summer times . . . I love her . . . (*Easy movement.*)

WOMAN: (*Rapid*) Brown eyes nice – hair dark soft – hands strong big . . . worrying thoughts . . . swimming nose, eyebrows, teeth, mouth – avaricious – devouring – like to be – now – who is he – what does he – how does he – bird-like – hawk-like predator . . .

MAN: The sea is calm today.

WOMAN: I like it like that – the way it churns in – chasing itself – not boiling or seething . . .

MAN: Dissolves on shingle as if grabbing with large tentacles . . .

WOMAN: A pile of coins – like coins slipping through its fingers as
　　　　it retreats . . .

MAN: Tentacles not fingers . . .

WOMAN: It moves – a wave moves like a mole under the water . . .

MAN: Or a rat under the carpet . . .

WOMAN: A long wave pushes, pushing until it collapses . . .

MAN: A fatigue of spume – spent froth white spume . . .

WOMAN: A long last gasp, phew!

MAN: Look at the sea! Like several hurdlers . . .

WOMAN: Racing – legs outstretched . . .

MAN: Relay runners, passing baton . . .

WOMAN: OH! Now they're collapsing.

MAN: The other runner is taking it – now he too collapses.

WOMAN: I like the sounds – lik-lak against the shingle.

MAN: He's sliding back into the arms of a dying wave.

WOMAN: They greet with much murmuring . . .

MAN: More a barely audible whisper – not close friends . . .
　　　　(*Pause.*)

WOMAN: I like the hurdler best – I can see that.

MAN: I like watching them race to the finishing line.

WOMAN: The sun's high in the sky – so heavy . . .

MAN: A fine breeze slides across our faces like cobwebs . . .

WOMAN: The sound of the sea is like whispered thunder . . .

MAN: Thin orgasmic little gasps . . .

WOMAN: That rock looks like a huge claw – frozen as if it
　　　　pounced on what it shouldn't.

MAN: Little wavelets bob and bow at its base.

WOMAN: Unctuous, spittle, boot-licking – toe-cleaning.

MAN: I thought I felt the earth shift.

WOMAN: It's a lovely day.

MAN: I think you're lovely – too. (*Aside*) HER BUTTOCKS ARE
　　　　SAILING ON TO MY HAND LIKE A TEA CLIPPER ON ITS
　　　　MAIDEN VOYAGE BOUND FOR THE ANTIPODES.

WOMAN: (*Shyly*) Strange thing to say on a beach – in your shirt
　　　　and necktie.

MAN: '. . . rich and modest, but asserted by a simple pin.'

WOMAN: 'They will say: "But how his arms and legs are thin!"'

MAN: 'Do I dare
Disturb the universe?'

WOMAN: 'In a minute there is time
For decisions and revisions which a minute will
reverse.'

MAN: My name is Thomas – Tom to you.

WOMAN: Oh, good – you could have been Bert – I'm so glad – I'm
Mary.
(*Silence*.)
You're not on holiday? What do you do?

MAN: (*Aside*) Desperate finger acrobatics . . . cruelly exposed
electric thigh encases, sheathed . . . my birthday present . . .
(*To her*) Selling mostly.

WOMAN: Mostly selling . . . ?

MAN: Space – mostly, I sell spaces of space, acres of nothing.

WOMAN: (*Disappointed – only a travelling salesman*) Oh . . . !

MAN: (*Aside*) She said – her face collapsing – rephrasing herself –
adjusting its concaves and shades – refocusing past me . . .
she crosses her legs, quick sound of surfaces abrasing –
signals of soft regions, the promised land . . . Boredom seeps
through – vinegar through milk . . . 'Oh!' – a collapse of the
lungs – expiration of interest.

WOMAN: (*Gentle tolerance*) I'm sorry – I didn't mean to sound
bored.

MAN: (*Quick aside*) She said, sounding bored.

WOMAN: More surprise really at selling nothing – how can you
sell nothing – a salesman sells something – he must do . . .
mustn't he? Something tangible – tactile?

MAN: I'm different, I sell the promise of something – the
intangible mystery of an empty space – pure white virgin,
untouched, waiting for a buyer to claim – to insert his
identity, his wares . . . his amazing declarations . . .

WOMAN: A trade book . . . ! A trade book! You sell space in a
trade book?

MAN: I promise trade in a space book.

WOMAN: How, promise?

MAN: When the book is full – when the white spaces are bought –
those infinite columns of expected wealth – I sell the book.

WOMAN: To whom?

MAN: To them – to the clients themselves, the space buyers, so
they can gaze at themselves immortalized forever in block
letters – electro-type on quarto double-weight.

WOMAN: Lovely!

MAN: Yes . . . when the space is bought we go to press – printing
blocks set up, letterpress, text, matter of context, put out
first proof, check it . . . supplement the appendix . . . print a
duodecimo for special customers then rush it out.

WOMAN: Exciting!

MAN: They open their books greedy yellow fingers . . .

WOMAN: Like fat worms?

MAN: Yes! Search for their spaces to see themselves described
forever in cuneiform characters – they like that . . .
Cigarette?

WOMAN: Thanks.

MAN: Do you want to buy some space?

WOMAN: Me?

MAN: How many of you are there? Yes, you.

WOMAN: (*Simply – wishing it were otherwise*) I have nothing to sell.

MAN: Hmmm . . .

WOMAN: *Have* I?

MAN: (*More edge*) Hmmm – you could have – find something –
everybody's got something – some one thing – even the
successful have got something . . .

WOMAN: All I have is a name.

MAN: That's all you need – sell that – have a half-inch single
column, just your name in uncial lettering – you'll excite
their imaginations – they'll create dream worlds containing
their idealized female – suiting every situation . . . you'll
fulfil their fantasies, become a mind-real, homogeneous.
Flickering through the hardware section they'll come to your
name sitting there like an unfulfilled hope . . . the ink of your
nomen stinging their pupils – gently grazing them with
mesmeric fantasies – they'll know you in a thousand different

ways and shapes, hundreds of colours, textures, smells . . .

WOMAN: (*Smiling*) My name will do that?

MAN: Their minds will do that – but your name, your explosive sibilant sigh will ease the first scab off those old love wounds.

WOMAN: I'm not sure – no, that I want those fat-fingered men dividing me up in their nasty abattoirs – taking me to pieces, examining me . . . imagining me . . .

MAN: You'll feel nothing – not even the tick under the skin as imagination catches desire by the tail.

WOMAN: I will, I'll sense . . . things . . . hundreds of little rays eating me up – my name belongs to me . . . I'll sense things – silent buzzes in the air – hovering invisible gnats . . . biting . . .

MAN: (*Quick aside*) Sensitive, sentient being, a mare trapped in a spider's web – a diastole in the heartbeat . . .

WOMAN: Revolting men, fat, wheezing behind desks in dirty offices . . . Ugh!

MAN: Clean mostly – sterile bright, shining world – the men fractured into brackets, parenthetically courteously explaining, or else in italics 'No, thank you . . . we've all the space we need, thank you, you're welcome, thank you . . .' At five o'clock the exodus – they stream out like diarrhoea . . .

WOMAN: You sound like high pressure – hissing from cracked pipes.

MAN: I'm no pressure – I dissolve into fat and slide under the door – staining the concrete stairs on the way down – those thousands of white – dirty – grey concrete stairs that have gnawed my feet away – choked on the dust – fine dust that concrete secretes – the salesman's disease – bang-bang, up the stairs then slither down in a visceral pool of grease dragging nerve endings, plasma and intestines . . . re-form on the pavement – plunge the eyes back in – the shirt has dissolved into my flesh – become an outer skin . . . Recoup in the ABC – salesman's filling station – pump in the hot brown bird vomit – the others are just sludging in, their faces slapped puce with rejection, the waitress, sliding around the

dead grease – falling apart at the seams, slithers her knotted
varicosity towards me and for a treat smashes some aerated
bread down my throat which dissolves into a dust, white dust
– like concrete dust, atrophying delicate nasal
membranes . . .

WOMAN: Don't you like your work?

MAN: Love it! Every moment, every earth-shattering
cosmological moment of it . . .

WOMAN: Even your dissolving agony?

MAN: That especially – you know the thrill of exploring this
fascinating city – meeting all those interesting people –
several square feet of flesh float up to you – not to you
directly but somewhere adjacent – dabbling in your
circumference . . . polite neatness glazes back at you, and *you*
shuffling sweaty lump – lift broken, spine snapped, eyes at
twenty-five watt, glint stumpy teeth, not exactly a smile
more a grimace of pain at the halitosis in your breath
escaping between your teeth like pistons . . .

WOMAN: (*Sickened*) I must go – but it's been nice talking to you.
(*She whisks herself past him. He jumps up and pins her violently
against the table.*)

MAN: (*Continuing*) . . . he may even buy some space to escape
your trajectory of rotting plumbing but usually the
protective secretaries have warned him of your arrival – 'He's
tied up, in conference' etc. – they nose you crawling up the
stairs – they're ready – alert as vultures . . . willing you out
but wanting to tear you to pieces – behind the door other
creatures are lurking, grey-faced salesmen with smiles
stitched on to their faces hovering like bats waiting for you to
go . . . Trembling lest you take an order . . . eyes bulging like
grapes . . . order books stained with dead egg yolk the
memory of which long since mercifully obliterated by some
tired old intestine . . . so I come here for an hour to look at
the sea, to escape from it – Oh, by the way, have a sandwich.
(*Opens his briefcase.*) They're really lovely, and you have a
choice – Oh come on, they're beautiful, made with my own
hands, which should add to the excitement . . . Go on please.

(*In persuading her he has spilt sandwich on her lap.*)

WOMAN: Oh dear – I've just had it . . .

MAN: Cleaned? Here let me . . .

WOMAN: No, don't, you're making it . . .

MAN: Worse? I'm terribly . . .

WOMAN: Sorry? Never mind – I must be off anyway.

MAN: Better still – have some soup – it's delicious like Grandma
makes it. (*Takes out bottle.*)

WOMAN: (*Rising*) No! Just leave me alone, will you?

MAN: Sit down! I'm not finished. (*Aside*) Tension's up, she's
become an ice lolly in a whirlwind.

WOMAN: I'm late.

MAN: Sit, animal. To heel! What is this, a cabaret? Go? Is that
what you do? Where are your manners – you call the act and
then walk out – what? You can't like the service? The
sandwiches? Me? All three? In that order – I'm not so bad
really, times are hard in the trade but things could be worse,
you could have done far worse, you should see some of the
casualties wandering around here playing pocket billiards,
but as long as you've got a pound in your pocket, you don't
have to ask anyone for nothing as my mother used to say . . .
a shine on your shoes, a nice cutaway collar on a van Heusen
shirt, you can sit in the Golden Egg, have a nice cup of
coffee, a chocolate éclair, hold your head up and be a
gentleman . . .

WOMAN: Goodbye then.

MAN: Aaaa . . . ! Wait

WOMAN: I'm late . . .

MAN: Please . . .

WOMAN: I don't want any space.

(*He collapses in chair.*)

MAN: What do you want?

WOMAN: Nothing.

(*He walks over and kneels at her feet.*)

MAN: I'm here.

(*He puts his hand over her calves – she does not move – they
remain silently.*)

WOMAN: No thanks – but thanks all the same.

(*She attempts to move but he holds her legs firm.*)

MAN: What's that mean?

WOMAN: No – that's what it means.

MAN: (*Imploring*) Two minutes more – I have something to tell you – marvellous wonders!

WOMAN: I've heard it – entertaining it's been – but I must go please – please let me go, please . . .

MAN: Don't you like me?

WOMAN: (*Weary*) Me . . . ? Like you . . . ?! Don't . . . !

MAN: What were you waiting for?

WOMAN: No one – I like sitting here – alone – that's how I like to be sometimes, I just sit here looking at the sea . . .

MAN: You were waiting! Yes, you were – I smelt your heat from across the beach. Your scent hung in the air like a pollen count – it commingled with the salty ozone and fish and sea, lost itself, but my quivering nostril located your particular waves – hound-dog-like sniffed it out, untangled it from the smell of fish and hamburgers fried, candyfloss, fags and dead sharks; located your special delicate whiff and zoned into it like radar. You were twitching for me, for somebody – yes you were – what did you expect, Gregory Peck? Or do you like the drama, the chat? It gives you satisfaction to be chatted to – sense of adventure – dallying with the mad unknown – weird stranger on the beach . . . picked up . . .

(*She attempts to go.*)

No, stay, you don't want to go back to that bare room, vinyl-lined, do you . . . ? Alone – rattling round four walls except for those flying ducks flight-frozen in dust, your frustration banging off them, the walls not the ducks, the street full of couples sliding happily across your windowpane past dead flies (feet saluting heaven) . . . and you pacing around waiting for the phone. So you come here for your adventures – to dispel the agony or share it.

WOMAN: I have a home and a husband and no agony to share – so let me go!

MAN: Ooh! A husband – but there's not the joy there was, eh . . . ?

227

So you compensate a little – inject the marriage with a
little spice to hold the structure together – I know how you
feel . . . the same body lying next to you night after night
after night – over and over again – it's sickening isn't it . . . ?
Search for the mad adventure of the first or second time
when you clawed each other apart as if you could discover, as
if you could wrench the secrets from that ticking body – oh
the terrible adventure of a first time . . . Hurtling yourself at
that marvellous machinery of joy – assaulting, exploring its
labyrinthine pleasure grounds . . . Satin-lined, lovely warm
corridors, armed with rubber teeth and special scented sauna
rooms and ice-cream parlours . . . Don't you wake up with
that snorting creature and for a second imagine that he could
be – something – one else . . . All this fantastic energy
burning holes in our stomachs – all this shock tissue dying
from unuse . . . Don't you ever want something else? Yes,
that's why you come here. Here I am for you – here you are
for me . . .

WOMAN: Nothing . . .

(*He walks over and kneels at her feet.*)

MAN: Here I am.

(*He puts his hands over her calves – she does not move – they
remain silently.*)

WOMAN: You're not looking for me – you're looking for *it*! Any it,
like a dog you sniff all the lamp posts . . . panting, licking
anything that comes your way, if it moves, sniff it, that's
you, you salesman of nothing, you canine groper.

MAN: (*Aside*) Calves hard as sculpture, warm as roses . . .

WOMAN: Wherever you drag your failure you leave a penetrable
whiff, a sour old fag smell – a whine, a hum of decaying
dreams and festering ambitions – it lingers in the air like BO.

MAN: (*Aside*) The blood's pumping – veins enlarging – shifting
masses in the flesh stir with life – the shoots begin to move –
the earth aches – the ache enlarges. THE EARTH BEGINS TO
SHIFT!

WOMAN: You demonstrate your wares like rotting garbage – you
woo like a leper – your expressions are the buried side of a

stone, moving with strange fetid life – dark, decayed, small scraping movements in the earth – odd creatures black and runny . . . or crawling . . . what the cat paws but carefully with distaste –

(*He puts his hands round her hips; holding her more and more tightly – she remains passive.*)

MAN: (*Aside*) Skulls pounding – a rat-tat-tat murder – blood soaks the brain, lids twitch and pupils dilate, skin stretches taut inside, everything taut, tight inside, outside – drums banging lubricious symphonies – trembling cadenzas – everybody take your partner – follow the rhythm, together – millions dancing the maniac jerk, the viscous spasm . . .

WOMAN: (*Not moving*) Take your hands away – your grimy, greedy little fingers – take them . . . *ay-way* . . . every pore a little hungry sucking nerve-centre drinking sensation . . . go away . . . your little slimy worms annoy . . .

MAN: I'm going – I'm going – I'm going, I am going . . . soon . . .

WOMAN: Now.

MAN: Soon – you *can* go – yes, you can go . . .

WOMAN: Now.

MAN: Soon, soon, soon – then you *can* go . . .

WOMAN: Now – now let me go – *please* now –

MAN: Soon, *please* soon – go soon – not now – not yet. (*Rising tone*) Not *now* – not *just* yet – not *so* soon . . .

WOMAN: (*Weakly*) You're defeating me!

MAN: No quarter – burst through . . .

(*Pause, during which she collects her strength for the climax – to hurt and be hurt. She beats him frantically.*)

WOMAN: Bite me. Bite snake! Bite loathsome! Draw blood – drink, drain me – you! You are a loathsome beast – searching and sniffing – your antennae alert as stretched tendrils – sensing out, sending waves creeping through the air, crawling stains of blood through laundered sheets . . .

(*He puts his hands round her neck and gently squeezes.*)

MAN: I want to murder you – draw your life out into me . . .

WOMAN: Murder me – you foul joy – you conquered repugnance!

(*Blackout. Music . . . the amplified sound of flowers opening.*

Their voices could be prerecorded.)

MAN: I tore into her body's haven
   ripped off rose-petalled flesh
   sucked from a host of seething fountains
   her sweet rich sanguine life

WOMAN: She said
   devour me all
   leave not one sliver
   not one small clue of silken down
   with tenderness he tore my heart out

MAN: Then bit into the puzzle of a frown
   imbibed, engulfed, devoured her . . . all!
   even her arms, long white and thin

WOMAN: No fragment left he of me sacred
   no faint opacity of skin
   not one square white unstained by him

   (*End of blackout. When the lights come up their clothes and
   physical state could suggest a swift fuck.*)

MAN: Anyway, so I suppose . . .

WOMAN: What do you mean?

MAN: It was nice . . . yes . . .

WOMAN: Nice . . . ? For who?

MAN: Not you . . . ? Not nice for you . . . you mean?

WOMAN: Like a fire engine, putting out . . .

MAN: A fire? You! A fire, *you*!

WOMAN: You died from exhaustion on the trek – you didn't rouse
   a twitch – or heat a pale flush . . . 'no quarter' 'burst
   through'! You couldn't burst through an ice-cream in a heat
   wave!

MAN: That black hole in your face squares into a tunnel of
   love . . .

WOMAN: You are a dirty little man.

MAN: Crawling words creep out like spiders from your ancient
   gob . . .

WOMAN: I do *believe* you dissolve into fat and slither under doors
   – you look like something that dissolved and recomposed
   with the bits and pieces off the floor – misshapen – lumpen –

that's failure for you – a man who can't sell nothing – or
make *something*!

MAN: Aah! What do you know you lump of fornicatory stew,
dolloping up bits of your overcooked goo . . . what do you
know! Who can linger on that – it . . . it (*Imagines her body –
miming*) falls apart in your hands – fingers don't find
resistance – strong, muscular, cellular resistance of filth-
packed flesh, no they just sink into you – loose masses of
wobbling, like a pack of dirty stories in aspic . . .

WOMAN: You're a real funfair comic – you're the woodlice that
one finds buried in bars telling the dirty stories you'll never
play in – stand in! Understudy!

MAN: Never play in?! I star in my own melodramas, long runs,
you one-night stand you!

WOMAN: I have a husband, I am to him, my husband, a veritable
drama of sensual events . . . that's what I am – a panoply of
exquisite variations . . . To him that's what I am, beside him
you dissolve – you're androgynous, on you it's an ornament!

MAN: Your husband never makes the love to you you think he
makes, but via you he is loving. Whilst you pant together
exchanging your sweat and stink, his imagination's taking
him to dreamland – you're just his launching pad, his
receptacle for his journeys into outer space where his dollies
lie waiting for him – his icy maidens fixed like cold glittering
stars ready to perform wonderful feats of endurance . . . but
wait until their light dies – just wait until then – because so
will you . . . a pack of memories, marriage . . . other
people's . . .

WOMAN: You are a poisonous spider – you really are . . .
poisonous. Yes, you even look like one – a crawling garden
spider, no not garden – the thing that darts out of dirty
cupboards, that you step on . . . FAST – yes, you do . . . My
husband loves me – yes he does – he loves me and soon it will
be time to go home and prepare his supper – he comes keenly
– lovingly in – expecting little kitchen noises and smells . . .
he brings the cold wintry air in with him . . . smelling of train
fumes and of Aqua di Selva – all fresh – a rough chin tickling

me, his smells reassuring me – all familiar. . . and he loves
me – really and hugely LOVES, and I make him his favourite
meals his mother once made him and we eat and watch TV –
not plays, or quiz shows, serious things, *Man Alive*,
Panorama – we discuss them afterwards and he writes long
eloquent letters to *The Times* about injustice – but they never
publish them . . . He's full of goodness – exudes it like
vapour – it clings to the walls of the room – every room . . . it
reaches into the grain of the furniture – becomes part of
them, part of me, so secure, cocoon-safe . . . six-ten each
evening, his tinkling key in the lock, his hat on the stand
faintly grease-stained – his himness coming in – hard,
masculine himness wrapping the house with blankets of love
. . . and just so he comes in the door, he whistles, so as not to
alarm me, so I know it's him – not anyone else, but him – not
a burglar or a murderer, a little whistle (*whistles three notes*)
and if I'm in the kitchen I whistle back so he knows I'm there
– not gone – not died – a victim of GBH or gang-bang angels
leather-winged – but there in a perpetual way, like he faces
me square on, direct and coming to me, always to me . . .
even when not facing me he's coming to me, his thoughts,
murmurs, hungers, desires, always reaching me and mine
him, so our invisible webs are always gripped even miles
apart . . . I finish his sentences, he collides with mine,
anticipate his wants – I don't need anything else – don't
certainly need you . . .

MAN: No – I'm not a whistling Aqua di Selva-ed square-on . . .

WOMAN: No – you're not square-on – you're oblique – you enter
from the side – or the back – like an unseen fist – one only
sees the shadow before impact, clenched malice – you –

MAN: No, malice clenched I'm not – a caressing angel more like.

WOMAN: A fist – all of you, a fist, to strike – you caress with your
fists to be ready – curled ball of furious venom – be anything
else, you couldn't.

MAN: I'm not a fist – my hands are soft – they caress – protect
DELICATE THINGS . . . Make flowers grow, life appear, make
people happy, women giggle, cats purr, dogs wag . . .

WOMAN: Goodbye then finally.

MAN: Goodbye.

WOMAN: Yes, goodbye.

MAN: Goodbye – go on . . . be home for six-ten – don't break your cocoon, soft-silky warm places should be protected – mad, you are, to be doing with me.

WOMAN: I'm sorry.

MAN: What sorry! Sorry that – sorry for . . . ? What?

WOMAN: Sorry – just sorry.

MAN: That's me, yes, oblique, the darting rat in the corner of your eye . . .

WOMAN: (*Encouraged*) Be careful . . . you're . . .

MAN: (*Showing his hand*) No fist – look (*A silence – he and she just look uncertain.* WOMAN *slowly takes one hand in hers.*)

WOMAN: You've uncurled . . .

MAN: The sea's stopped moving, the earth pauses . . . for a moment . . .

WOMAN: The tide has gone far out . . .

MAN: It begins to return, lovely, I think you are . . .

WOMAN: The sea is lovely and you . . .